MW00993779

 ALABASTER

© 2023 Alabaster Creative Inc.

All rights reserved.
No part of this publication may be reproduced, distributed, or transmitted in any form or by any means, including photocopying or other electronic or mechanical method, without prior written permission of the editor, except in the case of brief quotations embodied in critical reviews and certain other noncommercial uses permitted by copyright law. For permission requests, please write to us.

ALABASTER, the ALABASTER logo, and the trade dress of books in our Bible series are trademarks of Alabaster Creative Inc.

Unless otherwise indicated, all Scripture quotations are taken from the Holy Bible, New Living Translation, copyright © 1996, 2004, 2015 by Tyndale House Foundation. Used by permission of Tyndale House Publishers, Carol Stream, Illinois 60188. All rights reserved.

Scripture quotations marked (NIV) are taken from the Holy Bible, New International Version®, NIV®. Copyright © 1973, 1978, 1984, 2011 by Biblica, Inc.™ Used by permission of Zondervan. All rights reserved worldwide. www.zondervan.com. The "NIV" and "New International Version" are trademarks registered in the United States Patent and Trademark Office by Biblica, Inc.™

FSC
www.fsc.org
MIX
Paper | Supporting responsible forestry
FSC® C013123

Printed in Italy by Graphicom S.p.A.

Contact
hello@alabasterco.com
www.alabasterco.com

Alabaster Co. The Bible Beautiful.
Visual imagery & thoughtful design integrated within the Bible.
Cultivating conversation between art, beauty, & faith.
Founded in 2016.

 ALABASTER

The Good and Beautiful

Bible Study

VOL. II

An Introduction &
How to Use This Book

The Bible is good and beautiful. Its vast, historical recognition not only establishes its authority in our collective lives, but also shows us how its story and storytellers lead us to something bigger than ourselves.

Hearing stories has always deepened our understanding of our world. In early Jewish traditions, we see storytelling as a foundation for the flourishing of relationships, knowledge, and culture. Deuteronomy 11 (NLT) invites its audience to "commit yourselves wholeheartedly to these words" and "Talk about them when you are at home and when you are on the road, when you are going to bed and when you are getting up." These early traditions invite us to hear stories as an enduring, generational, and immersive experience.

This invitation from Biblical storytellers is often overlooked in our modern society. In today's contexts, it can be easy to reduce this ancient text to a set of brief take-aways, or moral to-do lists. But when we choose to see the Bible in this way we miss out on the fullness of what these stories can be—something wholly sensory and embodied.

We can look to early traditions of storytelling as a guide to engaging with the Bible today. The first communities gathered around sacred Bible stories, learning to embody those stories from generation to generation. Art has played a prominent part in this process, transmitting biblical stories and making them meaningful for each new generation. There is wisdom in following the steps of this method—noting how things transpire, and allowing them to speak, without rush or force. We used this as a guide in designing *The Good and Beautiful Bible Study* and invite you to engage with it two-fold:

READ	Whether it's heard aloud or in silent reading, hearing the story in its presented form is a bedrock for curiosity, conversation, and relationship.
I.	Each chapter's reading section opens with a **designated theme**, **synopsis**, and **reading list**. We invite you to begin your chapter experience by investigating these resources.
II.	The chapter then has an **outline**, retelling the story's events. To conclude the readings, we move into the **today** section, where we ponder the story and inspect its qualities and themes as they exist in our modern world today.
REFLECT	Through thoughtful curation of artwork, guided prompts, questions, and design, we invite you to integrate the story into the present and embody a full sensory experience. Looking to early traditions, we encourage gathering and sharing in this experience with others.
	Each chapter's reflect section is structured with prompts that will guide you through a process: Pause, Ponder, and Pray.
I.	*Pause:* Bring awareness to your response to the story. Each chapter has contemplative artwork and prompts inspired by the story's theme(s) to help guide you into the following steps below.
II.	*Ponder:* Deepen your understanding of the story with questions to reflect and/or discuss with your community.
III.	*Pray:* Close your time with a written prayer uniquely crafted for each chapter.
	We hope these promptings and works of art allow for a deeper experience with the Bible. Through your study, let there be joy, kinship, and an abounding connection with goodness and all of creation. Amen.

Vol. II

The One Who Delights in the Law of the Lord

The Story of The One Who Delights in the Law of the Lord

SYNOPSIS

A Psalmist offers metaphors for two paths of life—one of the blessed, who meditates on God's words, and one of the wicked, who commits wrongdoings.

> **KEY MOMENT:**
> Psalm 1

Read

Imagine a tree in the woods, firm and strong, planted on the bank of a river. This tree provides a home to any number of creatures. As the seasons change from winter to spring, the tree brings forth sweet and satisfying fruit. Passersby satisfy their cravings on their early spring walks. When summer comes, families flock to the tree for its shade and to swim in the adjacent river, bringing joy and connection to the woods and the larger community. In fall, its colors turn and bring a depth of beauty to all who lay eyes on it. And when winter comes again, it stands strongly through the storm, giving shelter to creatures who need it while preserving its energy for the following season of growth.

This is the path of one who delights in the words of God, who mediates on these words and creates space in their life for those words to take root. This blessed person provides shade and shelter for others, stands strong through the changing seasons, and offers joy, beauty, and connection to the world.

The same is not true for the wicked—the one who lives outside of the will of God. This person's life looks nothing like a tree that stands rooted in a space that can sustain it. Instead, they are like chaff—the discarded leftovers of a pile of grain. Chaff is inedible, and the slightest gust of wind will blow it away. It scatters and disperses, offering no value or sustenance to those around it.

This is the path of the wicked—taking advice from those who make bad decisions, going along with every wrongdoing done around them, and mocking those

CHOOSING OUR PATH

who try to do the will of God. Their path leads to eventual destruction—a judgment by God.

God watches over the diligent person who is like the tree, rooting themselves in the words of God. They are truly blessed and prosperous.

The psalms are an anthology of prayers, hymns, and other poetic texts, collected for use in Temple worship. They are multi-dimensional and deeply human: offering praise, lament, and all kinds of expression to God. The psalms come out of an authentic longing for connection to the Divine, a longing that connects us today to the world they were written in.

This psalm, like many others, is more descriptive of the world around us than it is prescriptive. We can look around and see the people doing their best to live in the way of love, joy, and peace—the way of God. The reality is not that they don't experience hardship—they have their winters, too—it's that they have a firm foundation and an environment around them that helps them remain strong and flourish throughout the years.

Likewise, we know people who continue to listen to those who don't have their best interests in mind, those who celebrate wrongdoings and mock those who strive to walk down the path of God.

While this psalm helps us see two types of paths we can choose to walk down, we can also acknowledge that life isn't always binary. The reality is that there are so many paths in front of us, and many of us zig-zag through life. We may find ourselves in seasons moving down a spiritually unhealthy path—but the grace of God can appear and reveal a trail back towards the Kingdom of God. The psalm serves as a guide—a reminder—of where we may find that trail back to God.

The wisdom of this psalm is more potent when we integrate the complexities of modern living—it's not always easy to practice the ways of God in our culture. There are so many distractions and cultural messages that run counter to the wisdom of God. Meditating on the words and ways of God can act as a compass that provides us with direction in an overwhelming society. Likewise, recognizing that we are handed so many different kinds of messages, this should help inspire compassion for others and the paths they take—their path will be judged by God alone at the right time. Instead of putting our energy into judging others' paths, we should strive to live a life that is truly blessed and rooted in the words and ways of God. This is the invitation of the psalmist.

In poetic, prayerful form, this psalm offers us a choice between two types of paths. Which path will you take?

The Grass Is Greener, Et Al.
BRYAN YE-CHUNG, 2022   OIL ON CANVAS

Reflect

PAUSE

Sit up straight.

Take a deep breath.

Using the art element (on the previous page),
take a moment to reflect on the story.

PONDER

Invite God to speak to you:

I.

What are the values that guide your life? What kind
of path are you currently on?

II.

How can you consistently use God's words to guide
you through difficult times and challenges?

III.

How can you extend compassion to those on paths
that are different from yours, knowing that their
path will be judged by God alone?

PRAY

God of Wisdom,
may we be like the tree,
firmly rooted in your words.
May we not be like the chaff,
scattered and swayed
by the path of destruction.
Guide us
amidst life's complexities,
and bless us
with abundant life.
Amen.

Struggle

Adam & Eve

The Story of Adam & Eve

SYNOPSIS

This famed creation myth culminates in curses against the snake, Adam, and Eve, and illustrate life's ancient and modern struggles.

KEY MOMENT:	FULL READING:
Genesis 3:8-19	Genesis 2–3

Read

OUTLINE

Genesis 2–3 covers the second creation myth in the book of Genesis. However, it is more than a myth about how physical creation came to be—it is a myth that describes how our struggles and our sorrows came to be as well. It illustrates both the beauty and the tragedy of life.

In this version, YHWH gathers dust from the ground and shapes it into the first human. God then plants a garden for the human to live in and care for. The human can eat the fruit of the land, except for the fruit from the tree of knowledge of good and evil—a form of knowledge we often describe as wisdom.[1] God sees that it is not good for a human to be alone, so God makes animals. Still, this is not enough, and God makes a second human, a woman, as the culmination of all of God's creative work.

In this garden, the two humans meet a snake, one of God's creations.[2] The snake convinces them to try the fruit, which will make them wise, despite God's prohibition.[3] The two humans seek wisdom—they desire to know good and evil for themselves; this desire for knowledge, for ancient readers, would have been understood as part of maturing out of childhood.[4] As soon as they eat the fruit, the two become aware of being naked, and they hide when God enters the garden. God questions the humans, and they proceed to pass the blame—from the first human to the woman and from the woman to the snake, perhaps implying that the blame lies with God, the creator of the snake.

STRUGGLE

[1] Genesis 2:17 / [2] Genesis 3:1 / [3] Genesis 3:6 / [4] Isaiah 7:14-17

Then God pronounces several curses. "Cursed are you," God says to the snake, which now will move on its belly, eating the dirt, and fearing the children of the woman. Perhaps the irony was apparent for ancient hearers. In the Hebrew Bible, winged-serpents called seraphim are God's attendants, but this snake now crawls and hides on the ground.

God says to the woman that her pregnancies will be multiplied, and they will be painful.[5] Part of the curse is also a dreadful state of patriarchy in which men will rule over her. God says to Adam, "Cursed is the ground because of you." Now, the once-fertile ground will produce thorns and thistles, and Adam will have to labor intensely to receive food from it.[6]

Both of the first humans' namesakes become tied to their sufferings. Adam is named after *Adamah*, the Hebrew word for soil or land, but now Adam suffers on account of the land, and the land suffers on his account. The one named after the ground itself is the cause of its curse. Furthermore, his relationship to the ground is strained. The woman is named *Chavah* (English: Eve) which sounds like the Hebrew word for life, *chayah*. She is named after life itself, but the process of bringing forth life will be painful and dangerous for her. The names of the first humans reveal how the beauty of land and life seems to have turned against itself.

[5] Genesis 3:16 / [6] Genesis 3:17-19

Snakes are cursed, humanity is cursed, and the ground is cursed. Genesis 3 is a challenging text for us. But this text is not about sin, a word never used in Genesis 3. Nor is it about a "fall," which is also not used in this chapter. This text is about feeling as if one lives under a curse.

Life was exceptionally hard in ancient Israel and Judah. The people struggled as subsistence farmers, and they relied on a rainy season that was notoriously unreliable. "Most males who survived early childhood typically lived into their mid-thirties, while most women died as early as their late twenties, half of them in childbirth." David Carr, a professor of the Old Testament, suggests that the curses of Genesis 3 adequately describe the hardships early Israelites faced in their daily lives. Ancient Israelites hearing this vivid story would have known women who tragically died too young, men who ruthlessly sought to dominate all others, and the challenging work of persistently farming arid land.

The blues standard, "Born Under a Bad Sign" by Albert King describes this feeling of being born cursed. The song starts with the words "Born under a bad sign, been down since I begin to crawl. If it wasn't for bad luck, you know I wouldn't have no luck at all." Like this song, Genesis 3 describes an experience of life's perpetual hardships. Creation experiences alienation from God, humans experience alienation from one another, and we collectively experience alienation from the land itself. Genesis even describes alienation from our very selves. These curses are not arbitrary, and they describe struggles still faced by us today.

Pregnancy still is incredibly dangerous for many women. Our "wisdom" and "knowledge" has both led to amazing innovation, but also to greater potentials for death and suffering. We have, through our wisdom, altered the earth itself, producing climate catastrophes and further alienating ourselves from the land which becomes increasingly less hospitable for all life. Producing food to feed humans remains a challenge across the world. Various states of patriarchy and gender-based dominance continue to persist with grave consequences. When we consider the experiences of our own lives and families, or witness the suffering of other people on the news or social media, or hear of impending catastrophes for our warming planet, it still feels as though we are cursed, "born under a bad sign." Genesis 3 would suggest that these are not intended states for creation, but curses which we should work against. Genesis 3 is a lament, not a prescription.

Briefly, let's consider one of the responses to the states of alienation we encounter. In Hosea 2, the prophet announces God's desire for salvation.

"On that day, an Oracle of YHWH,
You will call me 'my husband.' ...
I will make a covenant for them on that day,
With the creatures of the field, the birds of the air,
and the creeping things of the ground...
I will answer the heavens,
and they will answer the land.
And the land will answer the grain,
the new wine, and the fresh oil..."

Here, God announces a salvation. Rather than being alienated from the land, we will be brought into covenant with the land, with all the creatures of the air, land, and sea. And the land, rather than thistles, will answer with grain, wine, and oil. Hosea 1–3 also recalls the alienation experienced in human relationships and from ourselves, declaring that salvation will be the restoration of broken relationships between us. Salvation here is expressed in the exact terms of Genesis 3. This is a call to restore our relations with God, with one another, and with the earth and all its creatures. To participate in salvation is to restore our covenant with the land and with one another.

Sunburnt Nudes
JULIA SIGNE, 2021

OIL ON CANVAS

Reflect

Sit up straight.

Take a deep breath.

Using the art element (on the previous page), take a moment to reflect on the story.

PONDER

Invite God to speak to you:

I.

In what ways do the enduring curses of Genesis 3 still resonate with us and impact us today?

II.

Consider the passage from Hosea 2. What would a harmonious, peaceful world entirely removed from the curses of creation look like?

III.

How can we work against the curses of creation and bring about restoration in our relationships with God, one another, and the earth?

PRAY

God, help us restore
our bond with life and the land.
Help us alleviate the pain
of our curses.
May your promises
bring forth new life.
Save us, heal us.
Amen.

STRUGGLE

Ananias
& Sapphira

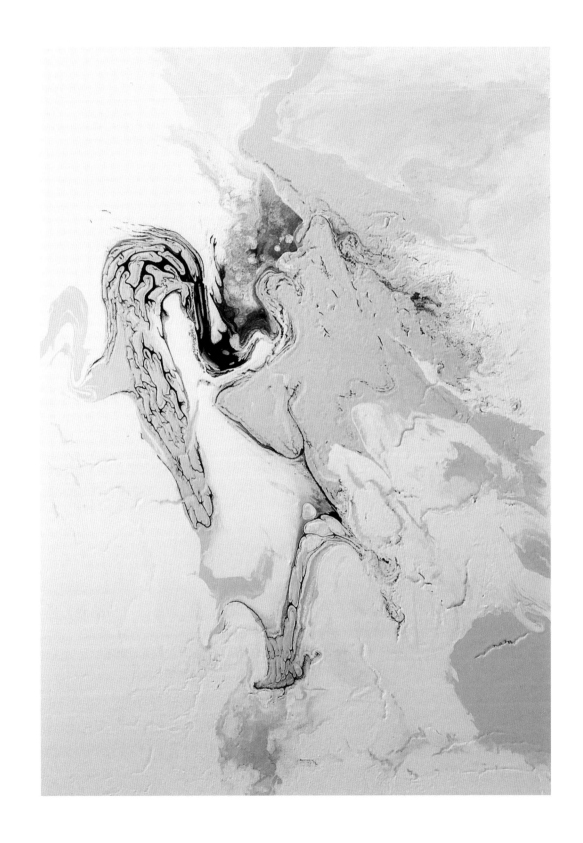

The Story of Ananias & Sapphira

SYNOPSIS

The tragic story of Ananias and Sapphira is about a couple who lies about their extraordinary gifts, an Early Church culture made up of people who give and share freely, and the deadly consequences of the couple's deception.

KEY MOMENT:	FULL READING:
Acts 5:1-11	Acts 4:32–5:11

Read

OUTLINE

When the Holy Spirit falls on Pentecost, people witness God's presence in a way they had not before.[1] After Peter proclaims the Spirit's pouring out on all flesh, many Jews repent, are baptized, and embrace a radical communal formation.[2] Many sell their possessions to support the common purse, from which all their needs are met.[3] Consequently, the church multiplies, and the easy flow of giving and receiving transforms people's lives. The haves and the have-nots find deep, meaningful fellowship with each other under the unifying banner of the Spirit.

One brother sells a property and brings all proceeds to the disciples.[4] So moved by his actions, they give him the name Barnabas, which means "son of encouragement." This name precisely affirms what the Spirit is doing throughout the entire community—encouraging them. Just as God compassionately provides Jesus for salvation, they generously offer resources to ensure that all material needs are met—boundless benevolence in action.

However, a husband and wife named Ananias and Sapphira see the attention given to Barnabas because of his gift and decide that they want to sell property and give a gift, too.[5] While we cannot be entirely sure of their motivations, we know that they only come forward after the disciples single out Barnabas' generous gift. Perhaps they think that if they gave more than Barnabas, they will receive new names and special recognition from the disciples as well.

But when they come with their gift, it is not the same as Barnabas'. Barnabas had brought all the proceeds

GIVING HONESTLY

from his sale. This couple only brings some of their profits, but present it as everything. We do not know why they did not offer the whole thing or why they were dishonest about only bringing a portion. Regardless of their reasoning, Ananias and Sapphira go through with the deception.

When the husband presents the gift, the disciples, filled with the Holy Spirit, ask the man why he let the devil deceive him; he does not just lie to them, but to God as well.[6] Instantly, he falls dead. A few hours later, his wife comes, and the disciples ask her if she and her husband had sold the property for the amount the husband brought. She solemnly says that they did, and right there, she too falls dead and has to be carried out, just like her unfortunate husband.[7]

The Spirit does not require people to give *all* they have, but the Spirit does expect honesty. In representing a portion as the whole, this couple prioritizes their desire for prestige and position over the transformative care the Spirit births into the community. This is the only passage in the New Testament where someone is struck dead by the Spirit. As the church witnesses their demise, it provokes fear. Given the structure of the story, we might distinguish how deception undermines encouragement. The community's generosity is a sign of encouragement. Ananias and Sapphira's duplicity leads to discouragement and death.

TODAY

A community like that in the first few chapters of Acts—marked by radical inclusion, hospitality, and generosity—encourages us. In our present context, so many of our communities and connections are

[6] Acts 5:3-4 / [7] Acts 5:7-10

mediated by social media. What makes social media so compelling is how it curates a portion of life as if it is the whole of life. Through our feeds, we select the bits of ourselves we want the world to see and long for the recognition that likes, engagements, and reposts offer. We are encouraged by these platforms to consume *portions* of peoples' lives and stories as the whole of their existence. Yet, on these platforms, we can too easily fall into patterns of deception about our actual lives. Instead of having our needs and vulnerabilities graciously met by a community, we can find ourselves isolated and unwell, with our community unable to encourage us when we need support—all because of a desire for popularity or recognition.

Nevertheless, God desires more for the church. The gift we have in the Church of Jesus Christ is to bring our *whole* selves, gifts, and liabilities—not because it is all beautiful, but because the Spirit promises to dwell in all of our flesh. Ananias and Sapphira could not trust that they were enough as they were. The more they centered themselves, the less they surrendered to the Spirit. God's transformation welcomes the vulnerability born in naming our needs and trusting the Spirit's desire to encourage us in communal generosity. We do not need more likes; we need the tangible witness of care. We do not need more reasons to fake it; we need space to come as we are.

While this passage highlights money as an object withheld, in truth, it can be any aspect of our lives that we deceitfully withhold from God and others. This story serves as a cautionary tale that represents the stakes of honesty with God and our communities. The invitation remains to give ourselves—but to do so honestly, in step with the Spirit, and for the benefit of the community we belong to.

Partie de l'âme
WESLEIGH BYRD, 2018   HOUSE PAINT, MEDIUM, ACRYLIC, ALCOHOL

Reflect

Sit up straight.

Take a deep breath.

Using the art element (on the previous page), take a moment to reflect on the story.

PONDER

Invite God to speak to you:

I.

In what area(s) of your life do you need to sincerely bring your entire self before God?

II.

How can we learn to trust in the Spirit? Where are we being invited towards vulnerability—whether by naming our needs or giving without reservations—to participate in communal generosity?

PRAY

God who knows all
and sees all,
receive all of me
as I am.
Grant me the freedom,
without reservations,
to trust in your goodness
when honesty invites me forward.
Amen.

Balaam

The Story of Balaam

SYNOPSIS

Balaam, a prophet, is hired to curse the Israelites. Instead, he delivers blessings, recognizing the power and impact of words.

KEY MOMENTS:	FULL READING:
Numbers 22:4-6,18-19	Numbers 22–24

Read

OUTLINE

Balak, the king of Moab, fears the Israelites as their numbers grow outside of Moab's borders.[1] He and other nations are deeply troubled; the Israelites have not moved through neighboring lands quietly. Now, these formidable, relentless people are at the doorsteps of Moab and the Midian people. Rather than face conflict, Balak seeks an alternative solution.

King Balak sends elders on a mission.[2] Armed with payment and instructions, they're to recruit the Moabite prophet Balaam to "curse the Israelites." Prophets at that time were divine mouthpieces—a curse from one could make all the difference socially and politically. In this situation, a curse could justify violent action and stoke fears surrounding the Israelites.

Balaam asks the visiting elders to spend the night while he earnestly seeks God's response to their proposition.[3] In the middle of the night, God visits Balaam and delivers a message that is the opposite of King Balak's fervent wishes.

"Don't go with them. Don't curse the people." So, Balaam refuses Balak's request to curse the Israelites.

Yet Balak is persistent. Instead of giving up, Balak sends more honorable emissaries with promises of unbridled fame, wealth, and power if the curse is uttered.[4] Upon their arrival, Balaam remains steadfast in his refusal. He invites these emissaries to spend the night intending to seek God's guidance once more before sending them on their way. But why would Balaam do this if God's command has already been spoken? Do the rewards promised by Balak have the prophet holding out for a different message from God so that he can cash in on his prophetic work?

The story takes a sudden turn. God tells Balaam to go with the emissaries to Moab. Thus, Balaam leaves first thing in the morning. But what makes this moment in the story even stranger is that in the very next verse, God is angry with Balaam for going![5]

On the road to Moab stands a messenger from God with a sword in hand, but only Balaam's donkey sees this figure.[6] The donkey refuses to go forward. Balaam, set on his destination, beats his donkey to get him back on track. This happens again and again as Balaam falls deeper into frustration. Ironically, Balaam fails to recognize God's involvement, misunderstanding the donkey's unusual behavior as a mere bother.

As Balaam beats his donkey a third time, God enables the donkey to speak, and it challenges Balaam. God then reveals the divine messenger, and Balaam finally sees. Contrite, Balaam offers to turn back if that is what is commanded of him. The angel tells him to proceed to Moab—but reiterates to only speak what he is told.

Upon reaching his destination, Balaam speaks God's words to Balak, bestowing blessings upon the Israelites and curses upon the people of Moab and Midian. Balak is left deeply disappointed.

TODAY

This peculiar drama invites us to reflect on the power of our words. Balak believes a strategically spoken curse can grant his formidable army an advantage against their foes. Balaam, on the other hand, is com-

⁵Numbers 22:20-22 / ⁶Numbers 22:23

mitted to speaking only what God commands him to—ultimately resulting in blessings for the Israelites and curses for Moab and Midian. The message is clear: God cares deeply about the words Balaam chooses and reaffirms the blessings for the Israelites.

We do not have to be kings or prophets for our words to carry weight. They need not even be audible. As Maya Angelou once said, "Words are things. You must be careful, careful about calling people out of their names…They get on the walls. They get in your wallpaper. They get in your rugs, in your upholstery, and your clothes, and finally into you." How we speak to our partners, our neighbors, and our coworkers has effects that can ripple out into broader communities. To a certain degree, all words contain prophetic power to bless or curse, to catalyze conflict or to cultivate peace.

So, are we consciously using our words to bless or curse others? If we have the urge to curse, could it be that God is trying to redirect our attention, gently reminding us of the right words to speak?

Our words have a communal dimension as well. Communication technologies not only increase the frequency and quantity of our words but can lock us into echo chambers and distance us from those who are affected by what we say. We need communities that we can trust with the intent of our words and that can advise us on their impact when spoken; people who remind us of the ramifications of hastily continuing down the paths of thoughtless speech.

As we strive for mindful communication, let us harness the power of our words, with every meaningful exchange, and bring forth a better world.

To Look / To Undergo
ERIN CLARK, 2021

LARGE FORMAT PHOTOGRAPHY

Reflect

PAUSE

Sit up straight.

Take a deep breath.

Using the art element (on the previous page),
take a moment to reflect on the story.

PONDER

Invite God to speak to you:

I.

How can we become more mindful of the impact
our words have on others and ensure that we use
our speech for good rather than harm?

II.

Has there been a situation in which you felt the
urge to speak negatively about someone? How did
you approach it then and would you do so now?

III.

In seeking understanding and empathy, how can
we actively redirect from echo chambers and move
towards people who have different perspectives?

PRAY

Dear God,
guide our words;
may they bless, not curse.
May we listen before we speak.
May we build up
a world of better words.
Amen.

POWER OF OUR WORDS

Bartimaeus

The Story of Bartimaeus

SYNOPSIS

Bartimaeus, a humble and blind beggar, unabashedly seeks mercy from Jesus and defies a world obsessed with wealth and status.

KEY MOMENT:	FULL READING:
Mark 10:46-53	Mark 10

Read

On his final pilgrimage to Jerusalem for Passover, Jesus continues to encounter many people with requests they believe only he can grant them. A rich man approaches Jesus asking what he must do to inherit eternal life—the one thing his money can't buy him. When Jesus tells him to sell everything he has and give it to the poor, the man walks away sadly, and Jesus teaches his disciples that those who are first will be last, and the last will be first.[1]

Jesus then begins to tell his disciples about his impending death at the hands of the religious leaders in Jerusalem. In response, two of his disciples, James and John, ask for seats at his right and left hand in glory. Jesus rebuffs them and teaches the twelve apostles that whoever wants to become great must become a servant.[2] Though Jesus had just taught something similar to the rich man, his disciples struggle to understand what Jesus is teaching—that the way of God is humility, servanthood, and mercy—not wealth, status, or power.

It's against this backdrop that we meet Bartimaeus. Jesus, along with many Jews, stays in Jericho as a final stop before Jerusalem. On this particular day, the road leading out of Jericho is an ideal spot for beggars and others in need to station themselves. Since God-fearing Jews are the ones making a pilgrimage, they might feel compelled to give money to the poor as a way to honor God. This is why we find Bartimaeus sitting on the side of the road.

Bartimaeus is a blind man. Levitical law says that a person bearing any defect, including blindness, would not be allowed to enter the presence of God in the

Temple and offer a sacrifice.[3] Therefore, he's excluded from the Temple, the crux of both religious and social life in the Jewish context. Numerous social structures have been established that leave Bartimaeus with no option but to beg from a spot on the ground.

With his cloak spread out before him, Bartimaeus hopes that people passing by will give enough money for him to cover his essential needs and survive. But today, the sense of hope feels different. Bartimaeus hears of this rabbi traveling around who heals people and speaks about the kingdom of God being close at hand. Both of these rumors energize Bartimaeus —the idea that he could be healed and the idea that a just God would come and rule in place of the corrupt government officials of his day. Somehow, through all the bustle on this busy road, Bartimaeus hears that Jesus is close. Bartimaeus calls out twice, "Son of David, have mercy on me," before the crowd tells him Jesus is calling back.[4]

Bartimaeus springs up and casts his cloak—the one he used to gather money—to the side. He follows the voices all the way until people tell him he is with Jesus. Jesus asks him, "What do you want me to do for you?" Bartimaeus responds, "Rabbi, I want to see." Then Jesus says, "Go, your faith has healed you." Immediately, Bartimaeus is able to see again, and begins to follow Jesus on the road to Jerusalem.[5] Though Bartimaeus was of a lower social status than the rich man and the disciples, unlike them, his request was granted, and he was invited into the kingdom of God.

[3] Leviticus 21:18-23 / [4] Mark 10:46-48 / [5] Mark 10:52

"God help the outcasts, hungry from birth. Show them the mercy they don't find on Earth. God help my people, we look to you still. God help the outcasts or nobody will." — *God Help the Outcasts,* Disney's Hunchback of Notre Dame

It's often the people we least expect who are able to demonstrate what the kingdom of God is like. Bartimaeus' story turns such expectations upside down. A wealthy man is unable to do what it takes to follow Jesus. The disciples don't understand the lessons Jesus taught. Bartimaeus may have been blind, but he was able to see in a way that the others couldn't.

The quote above is a prayer from Disney's Hunchback of Notre Dame. Esmeralda, a Romani outcast in her own city, demonstrates that she understands that the nature of God is mercy. The movie contrasts her with the churchgoers, who counter her song with their own refrain. In Esmeralda's story, it was the churchgoers that couldn't understand. In Bartimaeus' story, it was the rich man and the disciples. Whether they were clinging to their wealth or their perceived closeness to God—they still couldn't see the way of the kingdom of God.

Many of us might be tempted to hold onto power as a sign of God's blessing. We may have a job or a role that gives us a lot of social capital or respect from others—even before they get to know us. The story of Bartimaeus is a story of God seeing through the crowd of people vying for status and power, and choosing a person who seeks neither of these. God invites us to do the same. We too can become people of mercy, servanthood, and humility—and maybe then we can begin to see what Bartimaeus saw.

Blumentopf (groß)

AUGUST MACKE, 1913   **COLORED PENCIL ON PAPER**

Reflect

PAUSE   Sit up straight.

Take a deep breath.

Using the art element (on the previous page),
take a moment to reflect on the story.

PONDER   Invite God to speak to you:

I.   Consider the people in your life who exemplify the
virtues of mercy, servanthood, and humility; what
can you learn from their examples to cultivate these
values within yourself?

II.   In what experiences have you seen God's kingdom
values transcend societal norms?

III.   How can actively listening to and uplifting marginalized voices enrich your understanding of God's
love for all? How can you practice this today?

PRAY   God of Mercy,
help us to see like Bartimaeus,
to see beyond power and status.
Teach us
to be people of mercy
and to see all as
children of God,
loved and valued equally.
May we honor those in need.
Amen.

Recognizing Human Dignity

Bathsheba

The Story of Bathsheba

SYNOPSIS

Bathsheba—an innocent victim of King David's abuse of power—endures trauma, cover-up attempts, and heartbreak, but is seen and vindicated by God.

KEY MOMENT:
2 Samuel 11–12

Read

OUTLINE

One spring afternoon, Bathsheba is going about the routine business of life. The nation is at war and her husband, Uriah, a military leader, is away. In fact, most of the city's men are on the battlefront, and we are told that King David *ought* to have been among them.[1] Bathsheba's story begins with a bath, specifically, the religious purification rites that the law prescribed for women after menstruation.[2] Jewish law, according to Leviticus, gave guidelines on ceremonial cleanliness in this and many other circumstances. These practices were as much about spiritual purity as they were about physical hygiene.[3] All this to say, this was not a salacious or sexy task; it was just an ordinary and law-abiding activity.

Suddenly, messengers from the palace appear at her door, informing her that she has been summoned by the King immediately. Escorted from her home, Bathsheba finds herself face to face with David, the political ruler of the nation, the monarch divinely chosen by God. He wants to sleep with her and, given their difference in power and status, it isn't a request.

What began as a mundane day has become a nightmare as Bathsheba is raped by the King and promptly sent home to her empty house.[4] One can imagine how alone she must have felt in the aftermath of such a traumatic event with no one to confide in and no one to offer comfort or care. The situation then becomes further complicated when Bathsheba realizes she is pregnant.

RECOGNIZING HUMAN DIGNITY

[1] 2 Samuel 11:1 / [2] 2 Samuel 11:4 / [3] Lev. 15:19-30 / [4] 2 Samuel 11:4

She sends word to the King. David, her abuser and the father of her child, upon hearing this news is not remorseful. He offers no apologies for his behavior, nor any support to this frightened and lonely woman. Instead, David thinks only of himself and his reputation and immediately seeks to cover up what he has done.[5] He summons Bathsheba's husband home from the war, hoping Uriah will sleep with his wife and thus conceal the truth of David's actions with Bathsheba.

This scheming demonstrates that, king or not, David knows that his actions were wrong. God's hatred of rape and sexual abuse is explicitly stated throughout scripture.[6] The law of God is firmly on Bathsheba's side, but David uses his position of power, his responsibility as an arbiter of that law, to serve himself. His cover-up attempt seeks to erase his wrongdoing from the record. But Uriah refuses to go home to his wife while the rest of the soldiers remain on the battlefront. In desperation, David moves to plan B.

A short time later, more messengers arrive at Bathsheba's door, this time to inform her that her husband is dead, his death orchestrated by the King's own hand.[7] Struck with grief once more, Bathsheba cries out in

[5] 2 Samuel 11:6-13 / [6] Deut. 22:25-27 / [7] 2 Samuel 11:15

agony, mourning for Uriah. And once enough time has passed that he might avoid suspicion or public scrutiny,[8] David summons Bathsheba to the palace yet again where he takes her as *one* of his wives. Assaulted, bereaved, and forcibly uprooted from her home, Bathsheba soon suffers another heartbreak as the baby she has just given birth to dies.[9]

Through all of this, Bathsheba is continually dehumanized by King David. He objectifies her, and views her as a possession he can claim and control. She is stripped of her agency and her family. Her feelings, thoughts, needs, and wants are continually ignored in favor of David's own. But try as David might to erase the truth, God sees Bathsheba and is outraged by the injustices she has endured.[10] Refusing to allow David's crime to go unacknowledged, God sends Nathan to confront him. The violence enacted behind closed doors is brought into the open through David's public repentance and mourning for their son. Once relegated to bear the burden of her grief alone, her story is now told and recorded in Scripture, allowing us to grieve with her for generations to come. God recognizes her dignity and worth, that her name and her story are not forgotten.

TODAY

Reading about Bathsheba, we recognize the tragically familiar narrative of those in power preying upon the vulnerable—whether we know it from the news headlines or from the scars of our own experiences. In the face of trauma of this magnitude, it can be all too easy to lose sight of the real people at the centers of these stories. We are often left with nameless victims and survivors who are glossed over and ignored due to our own discomfort. Their stories and experiences are frequently erased and silenced, or else essentialized as talking points—people turned into emblems of a cause.

Bathsheba herself often falls victim to this kind of commodification. A cursory reading of 2 Samuel 11 and 12 often leaves us with a picture of Bathsheba as more of a narrative device in David's story than a fully fleshed-out character in her own right. But Bathsheba was more than a plot device. She was a woman of faith, a community member and citizen, a wife and mother with a full life to live—a complex human being made in the image of God.

The echoes of Bathesheba's circumstances are unsettlingly similar to the power dynamics and abuses of today. In the last decade, in particular, we have seen those in power—studio executives, CEOs, priests, politicians—take advantage of their positions and

RECOGNIZING HUMAN DIGNITY

the systems they oversee to prey upon the vulnerable. Story after story of sexual abuse shows how often human dignity is disregarded.

Bathsheba's story assures us that these abuses of power anger God. What victimizers seek to conceal and hide, God brings out into the light.[11] Movements such as #MeToo and #ChurchToo reflect this refusal to let harassment and assault remain unacknowledged. As countless victims and survivors came forward to share their stories, a culture wake-up call was sounded, demonstrating the scope and scale of this problem and declaring that things need to change. Alongside this commitment to justice, God also sees the individuals affected by the transgressions of the powerful. Our worth is intrinsic to who we are as beloved creations of God. Bathsheba has value, and each of us has value, beyond what we are able to achieve or offer.

God ensures that stories of injustice are not forgotten or sanitized, urging us to confront, acknowledge, and reckon with the realities of trauma and lament. To fully engage the story of Bathsheba is to sit with her in the reality of her pain, fear, and grief. It is to recognize that God compassionately meets us there in the midst of the mess and confusion.

Zion
JACKIE TAM, 2022   **SUMI INK ON YUPO PAPER, DIGITAL COLOR**

Reflect

PAUSE

Sit up straight.

Take a deep breath.

Using the art element (on the previous page),
take a moment to reflect on the story.

PONDER

Invite God to speak to you:

I.

In what ways are power dynamics and abuses of
power still manifested in our society today?

II.

What steps can we take to create a culture that values the dignity and worth of all individuals?

III.

How can we turn to God in times of distress, and
allow God's presence to bring healing and hope?

PRAY

God, help us see.
May we never forget
that You see us in our pain
and meet us in the mess
with abounding love.
May we work for justice,
the oppressed,
and the worth of all people.
Amen.

RECOGNIZING HUMAN DIGNITY

The Bleeding Woman

The Story of The Bleeding Woman

SYNOPSIS

A woman with a long history of bleeding musters all her courage to touch Jesus' cloak, and is healed both physically and socially by his compassion and affirmation.

> **KEY MOMENT:**
> Mark 5:21-42

Read

OUTLINE

"If I touch his clothes, I will be healed."[1] The woman repeats it to herself like a mantra.

She sees that Jesus is on his way to the home of Jairus, the rich and powerful synagogue ruler.[2] The large crowds that press in on Jesus from all sides[3] have parted—just a little bit, but unmistakably so—when Jairus rushes to Jesus' feet and begs for healing for his dying daughter.[4] No one is surprised when Jesus agrees to go and help this very important man.[5]

It is clear that Jesus is on an urgent mission. As the woman approaches him, she knows it will be awkward, unexpected, uncouth. It will call forth all the courage she has. "If I touch his clothes, I will be healed." Her desperation overrides her fear.

She has tried everything,[6] but the blood flow has always been with her—not just a few days every month, but twelve long years,[7] and so much blood that it brought to mind a spring of water. (The Greek word used here, *pēgē*, refers elsewhere to a fountain or spring.)[8]

The woman had always been considered unclean; she was always excluded from religious services and from full participation in community life. And she was tired, so tired. As the blood continued to drain out of her, so did her energy. The doctors had taken her money but had not helped her.[9]

But then she hears about Jesus, the man who heals people who cannot be healed. There is something special about him. "If I touch his clothes, I will be healed." It takes courage to believe.

COURAGE / DESPERATION

---

[1] Mark 5:28 / [2] Mark 5:22-24 / [3] Mark 5:21, 24, 31 / [4] Mark 5:23 / [5] Mark 5:24 /
[6] Mark 5:26 / [7] Mark 5:25 / [8] Mark 5:29 / [9] Mark 5:26

She pushes through crowds who do not make way for her. Finally, she is there, right behind him. She reaches out and touches his cloak,[10] and she feels something change inside her. The bleeding stops immediately. She knows in her body that she is free from her suffering.[11]

Jesus knows, too, but he does not want to leave her healing incomplete. She is physically healed, but not yet socially or relationally restored. This restoration takes a different kind of courage: the courage to be seen.

"Who touched my clothes?" Jesus asks.[12] His disciples think the question is ridiculous. "You see the people crowding against you, and yet you can ask, 'Who touched me'?"[13] But Jesus doesn't give up, and the woman comes forward, falling at his feet just as Jairus has done. She trembles with fear but speaks up anyway, telling Jesus everything:[14] all the years, all the blood, all the doctors who did not help, all the impoverishment trying to get well, all the disappointment, all the exclusion, all the pain.

In response to her fears—and her courage—Jesus speaks words of comfort: "Go in peace." He speaks words of affirmation: "Daughter, your faith has healed you." He speaks words of liberation: "Be freed from your suffering."[15] Everyone hears these words. Everyone knows her, now, not as the unclean one, but as the healed one—and as the one whose faith Jesus admires.

In her courage to press through the crowds that paid no attention to her, the woman is healed in her body. In her courage to speak up and tell her story, she is restored in her community.

[10] Mark 5:27 / [11] Mark 5:29 / [12] Mark 5:30 NIV / [13] Mark 5:31 NIV /
[14] Mark 5:33 / [15] Mark 5:34

For some of us, courage might feel like it is in short supply. But courage is not necessarily a feeling of bravery. It is certainly not a posture of bravado. Sometimes, courage, for us—like the woman in the story—is simply born out of desperation. We can grow more courageous over time through each seemingly small, brave choice we make.

It takes immense courage to actively pursue personal, relational, and societal healing. God gives us a vision for healing and reconciliation, both for the suffering in our own lives and for the injustice in our world. This vision makes us brave.

For us, like the woman, sometimes courage means choosing to face our pain. We might find this terrifying, and that is okay. Acting with courage does not mean living without fear. We can take small, doable steps forward—in the midst of our fears—to acknowledge the difficult things in our lives and our world, facing them and not running away from them. We can see what possibilities for healing might appear as we do so.

As Brené Brown writes, we can "find the courage to own the pain" of our own experiences of exclusion and in so doing, "develop a level of empathy and compassion for [ourselves] and others that allows [us] to spot hurt in the world in a unique way."

With the courage to face our pain, we often find empathy and compassion. We gain insight into the hurt experienced by others around us, and we become part of the healing of our world. Whether or not we feel particularly brave, God invites us—like the woman—to make courageous choices toward justice, healing, and peace. God is with us, strengthening us with vision and purpose as we do so.

Red Sunset on the Dnieper

ARKHIP IVANOVICH KUIDZHI, 1905-1908   **OIL ON CANVAS**

Reflect

PAUSE   Sit up straight.

Take a deep breath.

Using the art element (on the previous page),
take a moment to reflect on the story.

PONDER   Invite God to speak to you:

I.   Where do you draw courage from? How can you
cultivate more courage through small daily steps,
even in desperate situations?

II.   In what ways can acknowledging and facing the
difficulties in your life and in the world lead to
healing possibilities?

III.   How can owning your own pain help you develop
empathy and compassion for others?

PRAY   God, help us find courage
every new day.
Give us insight
into our wounds,
and compassion
for the world's pain.
May healing and justice
abound today and tomorrow.
Amen.

Boaz

The Story of Boaz

SYNOPSIS

Esteemed Boaz unexpectedly finds Ruth gathering leftovers in his fields and—amidst cultural barriers and societal norms—seeks a radical way to provide safety.

KEY MOMENT:	FULL READING:
Ruth 2:4-12	Ruth 1–4

Read

Boaz, a wealthy man from Bethlehem, meets Ruth when he is making the rounds, checking on his land and his crew of field workers. He sees Ruth working behind his men, and her hands are scratched from gathering scraps of grain.[1] She's been allowed to follow the professional harvesters and collect leftovers, as was the custom for poor widows.[2] Boaz asks one of his workers about her, but then Boaz breaks social norms, looks directly at Ruth, and tells her to stay in his field. He tells her she will be safe on his land. He also speaks a blessing over Ruth, telling her that he heard she is caring for her widowed mother-in-law, Naomi. He calls her truly blessed and praises her for actively seeking protection from God.[3]

While we know from the rest of this story that Boaz and Ruth eventually marry—this interaction is not about love at first sight or inflated infatuation; instead, it is rooted in honoring the outcast as a way of honoring God. The backbone of Boaz's behavior is rooted in keeping the God of Israel at the center of his life. Instead of saying, "I'm being nice to you because God has blessed me with riches," Boaz attributes her protection and safety entirely to God.

His kindness confuses Ruth.[4] She isn't sure why someone with his social status is being kind to her—not only is she poor, she is also an immigrant from Moab. The men of Israel had been warned not to marry Moabite women, so Boaz is crossing cultural, economic, and religious boundaries by showing kindness to Ruth. And the kindness continues.

[1] Ruth 2:1-3 / [2] Leviticus 19:9-10 / [3] Ruth 2:8-12 / [4] Ruth 2:13 / [5] Ruth 3:7-9

When Naomi hears that Boaz treated Ruth well, she tells Ruth to risk everything and ask for more generosity from him. Boaz goes to sleep in the room where the grains are stored, but he wakes up to a sound. When he sees Ruth at his feet, he is shocked.[5] Naomi had told Ruth to go to him at night and present herself, but Boaz doesn't know this. This is nontraditional behavior at best, and outrageously scandalous at worst, but Boaz knows he can trust Ruth. Boaz stays true to his commitment to obeying God and chooses to protect her. He tells her he will provide for her and protect her by marrying her and that he just has to sort out a few business details. (Boaz wasn't the first in line to marry Ruth; widows were supposed to marry the next closest relative after their husbands died.) Boaz handles the "paperwork" with Ruth's closest male relative, and then he arranges to marry her.

They have a baby boy named Obed, who ends up being Kind David's grandfather.[6] The people of Israel had one of their greatest kings—King David—because Boaz decided to marry a Moabite. From Boaz's behavior we learn that everyone is not just included, everyone is *needed* in order to fulfill God's plan.

TODAY

From this story, we learn that God will work powerfully in and among the people we might least expect. The story of Boaz is found in the Old Testament Book of Ruth. The writer is unknown, but their motive was clear. They wanted to provide a backdrop for the upcoming story of King David, and they wanted to highlight the power of welcoming immigrants as part of God's people. This is a short, yet powerful, story of love. This love, however, didn't begin with infatuation or clumsy meetings we so often associate

[5] Ruth 3:7-9 / [6] Ruth 4:9-17

with love stories—it began with a love for the outcast. Boaz's first action when he met a poor immigrant working in his fields was to give God credit for her protection and provision; then, he used his own hands and resources to join her in her search for food and shelter. He wasn't absorbed by power, and he knew he was partnering with God to give Ruth food security and physical safety. The credit was God's, but Boaz saw himself as a participant.

Boaz shows us that the family of God is open to anyone, but he takes it a step further. He shows us that the least likely person can also become a leader. It is through the incorporation of Ruth into the family line of King David that we see the mystery of the Kingdom of God—it is expansive, all-encompassing, and inclusive, all because Boaz knew that God's work extended beyond the people of Israel.

We may find similarities with Boaz in our lives as we consider our jobs and homes. Many around us have less, and Boaz's actions provide a guide for using our resources, such as time, energy, and money, wisely. Instead of hoarding, he kept his land open, allowing the needy to glean. Actively supporting their humanity, he built relationships with them. This mindset shift can reshape our perspective towards unhoused or undocumented neighbors.

Even if we might not have the resources to buy someone a house, we can still look people in the eye and show them respect. We can choose to interact with them instead of look the other way. We don't need a ton of extra money to be considered someone with power in our society. Boaz shows us that even our attention and friendship can be powerful tools that help us live with those around us.

Måker
JULIA SIGNE, 2022   OIL ON CANVAS

Reflect

PAUSE

Sit up straight.

Take a deep breath.

Using the art element (on the previous page),
take a moment to reflect on the story.

PONDER

Invite God to speak to you:

I.

How can we use our resources wisely to actively
support those in need?

II.

Consider your daily rhythms. Are there routines
in which you can make more space to be present
to those in need around you?

PRAY

God of the outcasts,
guide our path
towards Your way.
Nurture our love,
and may we embrace others,
act generously,
and honor You.
Amen.

Caleb

The Story of Caleb

COLLECTIVE LIBERATION

SYNOPSIS

Caleb and his people navigate challenges—on their arduous journey toward the Promised Land—in pursuit of collective liberation.

KEY MOMENT:	FULL READING:
Numbers 13	Numbers 13–14

Read

In the wilderness of Paran, Caleb and the Israelites follow Moses on a journey towards the Promised Land, seeking collective liberation after years of subjugation. However, because the journey is long and difficult, many begin to doubt and become cynical, wondering why they chose to follow Moses in the first place. After all, if they had stayed in Egypt they would still have the security of food and shelter as opposed to being exposed to the dangers of the desert. Despite this, they press on towards liberation.

As they draw closer to the land of Canaan, Moses sends one representative from each tribe of Israel to go and scout the land.[1] Caleb is sent as one of these spies from the tribe of Judah. At the end of their scouting, Caleb and the other spies return to Moses with a report about the land. They bring back delicious fruits of pomegranates and figs, showing the lush harvest the land can provide. It is indeed a land flowing with milk and honey.[2]

However, the land has other people living on it. The land is completely occupied by some of the most feared tribes known for their strength and size. The people who occupy the land have also fortified it with walls to protect themselves, preventing immigrants from intruding on their land's bounty.[3]

The Israelites grow discouraged; they have suffered so much, traveled so far, and are now being prevented from crossing into this land of opportunity. But Caleb, longing to see God's promises fulfilled, remains confident in God. While the reports from some spies cause fear among the people, Caleb boldly speaks up, saying, "Let us immediately go and occupy the land,

COLLECTIVE LIBERATION

I know we are able to overcome any obstacle that may present itself!"[4] Caleb, remembering the miracles that brought them out of Egypt, maintains his faith that God will make a way forward.

Most of the Israelites want to go back to Egypt, as they are too scared to go any further. Why would God put them in this precarious position? Are they being led away from oppression in Egypt just to be slaughtered by the sword in Canaan? Hearing these fears, Caleb, Joshua, and Moses tear their clothing in an act of distress. They cry out, pleading with the Israelites to reconsider God's promises.

Miraculously, God appears and defends the cause of Caleb, Joshua, and Moses. God chooses to bless their steadfast faith.[5] To those who are cynical and pessimistic, God threatens them with disinheritance. For those who are faithful, God blesses them for generations to come. Caleb's faith is founded on the fulfillment of God's providence seen time and time again. Caleb has witnessed the liberation of God as a former slave in Egypt, and Caleb knows that God would not have led them so far without bringing his people freedom.

TODAY

Collectively, Caleb and his people had experienced trauma, oppression, violence, and degradation. They witnessed unimaginable moments—they fled from slavery, were hunted down, and witnessed more miracles that allowed for their escape from slaughter and captivity. Caleb shared in the collective trauma of his own people and held steadfast to his hope in God. Even in the face of supposed giants, Caleb believed in God's promise.

What is true for Caleb can be true for us. Through history, we see this same cycle continue to take place. There

[4] Numbers 14:6-9 / [5] Numbers 14:20-24

have always been institutions and rulers who seek to oppress. Even ordinary life is full of every-day obstacles and giants that may seem impossible to overcome. We may be struggling with insecurities, depression, addictions, etc. God seeks to liberate us from these things as well. The Bible shows that God is always on the side and cause of the disinherited. God is always seeking to liberate the afflicted from all that harms them.

Caleb confidently saw God's aid in overcoming adversity for the Israelites. Despite their cynicism, he firmly knew God would liberate them.

A beautiful part of Caleb's story is the way in which he lived out his faith in community and remained with that community—even in disagreement. Many of us have grown up in traditions that emphasize faith as an individual experience. Despite Caleb providing a different report than most of the other spies, he remained with his people through the duration of their journey in the wilderness. Just like his appeals to their common history and experiences, he maintained a hope for a common future for the next generation. To Caleb, faith is a communal experience—they were enslaved as a collective and could only be liberated as a collective.

We can be like the other spies who grew cynical or, like Caleb, we can place our hope in the God who wants everyone to find liberation. We can chart an individualistic course to get there, or we can continue to persevere in our communities, even among disagreement. Although a solo path may feel satisfying in the moment, no one is truly liberated until we are all liberated. We too have been invited to a collective and communal liberation. Together, through disagreement and doubt, we can forge a path forward together to see God's promises fulfilled.

Moondance

COLT SEAGER, 2022

OIL ON SEWN CANVAS

Reflect

PAUSE

Sit up straight.

Take a deep breath.

Using the art element (on the previous page),
take a moment to reflect on the story.

PONDER

Invite God to speak to you:

I.

How can we, like Caleb, maintain hope and trust
in God during times of widespread adversity?

II.

In what ways can we nurture a sense of together-
ness in our communities when disagreements arise?

PRAY

God,
in our pain,
and trauma,
we've faced many giants.
May we find strength
in community
and find liberation together
through Your power.
Amen.

Balancing Desire With Wisdom

David
& Absalom

The Story of David & Absalom

SYNOPSIS

King David faces moral dilemmas, while his son Absalom's thirst for justice and power leads to a tragic, explosive confrontation.

KEY MOMENT:	FULL READING:
2 Samuel 18	2 Samuel 13–18

BALANCING DESIRE WITH WISDOM

Read

As the prophet Samuel's advice echoes in their ears, the people of Israel grapple with a critical decision on who should lead them. Should they place their faith in Yahweh, the God who freed them from slavery, or in judges like Deborah and prophets like Samuel? Or, should they entrust their fate to a divinely appointed king? Samuel suggests appointing no king; they should trust in God alone.[1] Nevertheless, the people want a human ruler that comes from earth. God ultimately selects a king—David, the second King of Israel.[2]

Israel's first king, Saul, breached his covenant with God, losing divine favor by disobeying an order to vanquish the enemies of Israel.[3] Surely, King David, a "man after God's own heart,"[4] could do better? Yet, even the devout David struggles with internal conflicts that threaten his kingdom, and he often overlooks the wise counsel of his advisors. Immediately prior to our story with David and Absalom, in the grip of desire, David spies on Bathsheba and engages in a scandalous affair.[5] Disregarding morals and wisdom, David orchestrates her husband's death to conceal his misdeed.

Absalom, King David's son, seethes with a desire for power that corrupts and devastates any relationship in its path. Driven by this burning passion, he commits treason, capturing Jerusalem, Israel's capital, and u-surping the throne.[6] But what propels him to betray his own father? Why would he betray blood for power?

The story unravels, revealing prior to this conflict that Absalom's actions were fueled by a hunger for justice.[7] His sister Tamar had been raped by David's other son, Amnon, and David's failure to hold Amnon accountable ignites an inferno of dysfunction within

[1] 1 Samuel 8:10-18 / [2] 1 Samuel 16:1-13 / [3] 1 Samuel 15 / [4] 2 Samuel 13:14 / [5] 2 Samuel 11–12 / [6] 2 Samuel 15 / [7] 2 Samuel 13

the family. As the flames grow, Absalom can no longer bear the searing pain of injustice and neglect. He, too, disregards the advice of his trusted advisor, Ahithophel, which eventually leads to his defeat.[8]

The conflict spirals out of control and hurtling towards a final, explosive showdown for the throne—a dramatic battle that fiercely pits father against son.[9]

Before the battle, David wrestles with his conflicting desires—he longs to preserve his kingship but is desperate to protect his son's life. David instructs his commander to leave Absalom unharmed, but as the battle rages, Absalom meets a gruesome and dramatic end at the hands of David's army.[10]

Upon receiving the news, David crumbles beneath the weight of his grief. Despite his victory, the story reads: "The king was shaken. He went up to the upper chamber of the gateway and wept, moaning these words as he went, 'My son Absalom! O my son, my son Absalom! If only I had died instead of you! O Absalom, my son, my son!'"[11]

TODAY

We sometimes crave what harms us—a challenging truth in the human experience. King David was captivated by the lure of power and its privileges, while Absalom sought justice but ultimately succumbed to a similar hunger for power. Both father and son were blinded by their desires and disregarded the wisdom that could have helped mend their relationship, ultimately leading to them suffering the consequences.

BALANCING DESIRE WITH WISDOM

[8] 2 Samuel 17:1-14   /   [9] 2 Samuel 18:1-18   /   [10] 2 Samuel 18:5-17   /   [11] 2 Samuel 18:33

Upon self-reflection, have our desires ever led to pain? It could appear as pursuing a promotion, only to find ourselves swamped by tasks, losing touch of what matters. Or, it might manifest as a pursuit of a passion project, in which we unintentionally sideline loved ones, strain relationships, and foster resentment.

Desire itself is not inherently negative, but when we don't incorporate wisdom into the mix, it can be harmful. Absalom's desire for justice wasn't wrong, but without wisdom guiding his pursuit, he spiraled into a lust for power and domination. David's desire to reconcile with his son was admirable, but without wisdom to guide and inform his actions, he inadvertently led Absalom to his death.

The path of wisdom demands that we slow down, reflect inwardly, and communicate honestly and fairly with others. Like water gradually smoothing the rough edges of a stone, wisdom diligently guides our desires, helping us pursue them in a harmonious and balanced manner. So much heartache and loss could have been prevented if David had applied wisdom to his interactions with Amnon. If Absalom had paused to reflect carefully, he might have discovered compassionate others who could have shown him how to seek justice non-violently. If David had taken a step back, he could have brokered peace with his son.

We need not fear or stigmatize desire; instead, we are invited to integrate our desires with wisdom for ourselves and those we care for deeply. In doing so, we can create a more harmonious and fulfilling world— the one we all truly seek.

In den Dolomiten

MEDWARD THEODORE COMPTON, 1870-1880   OIL ON CANVAS

Reflect

PAUSE

Sit up straight.

Take a deep breath.

Using the art element (on the previous page),
take a moment to reflect on the story.

PONDER

Invite God to speak to you:

I.

Reflect on a time when your desire for something
may have clouded your judgment. What lessons
did you learn? How have you grown as a result?

II.

How can we incorporate wisdom to help guide our
endeavors? In our daily life?

PRAY

God,
guide our hearts
in wisdom
as we navigate
desire's dance
with love
and grace.
Amen.

The Disciples and Jesus

D.Kakabadzé. 1921.

The Story of the Disciples and Jesus

SYNOPSIS

The dismayed disciples go fishing but end up catching nothing. A risen Jesus calls out from the shore and, over a charcoal fire and a meal, restores their relationship and partnership.

KEY MOMENT:
John 21:1-14

FULL READING:
John 21

Read

After Jesus' death, Peter and the disciples return to what they knew best: fishing.[1]

However, their fisherman's instincts do not produce the results they had hoped for—their nets yield nothing. Imagine their dismay: their friend and mentor, Jesus, has just died, and they are afraid, ashamed, disheartened, and frustrated. Now they are exhausted from fishing all night with no results.

Suddenly, as morning comes, a lone figure appears to them on the beach, calling out affectionately, "Children, you have no fish, have you?" Following this fleeting, mysterious interaction with the stranger, their nets transform from being empty to brimming with fish to the point that they strain to haul it all onto their boat![2]

Peter recognizes this abundance as a miracle—it is a callback, inextricably linking this moment to their earliest experiences with their Rabbi. The stranger calling to him is Jesus! Peter, overjoyed, swims excitedly to shore while still wearing all his clothing.

As the disciples reconvene on the shore, Jesus is already waiting with fish cooking over a charcoal fire, and he invites them to include their catch in the meal.[3] A small but significant detail to this passage is the charcoal fire. The only other time a charcoal fire is mentioned in the Gospel of John is during the events leading up to Jesus' crucifixion.[4] Peter and others had gathered around this fire, and as Peter is recognized as one of Jesus' disciples, he denies knowing Jesus three times.

HEALING AND RESTORATION

[1] John 21:3 / [2] John 21:4-6 / [3] John 21:7-10 / [4] John 18:18

Now, huddled around a crackling charcoal fire once more, Jesus turns to Peter. With tender concern in his eyes, Jesus gently asks Peter, "Peter, do you love me?"

Peter, sensing the question's gravity, answers earnestly. "Yes, Lord, you know I love you."

Jesus and Peter converse back and forth over this significant question three times.

This is a restorative and reconciling moment that mirrors the instance in which Peter had denied Jesus three times. A sense of grace is present. As the relationship between Jesus and the disciples is restored, so too is the mission: to "feed [his] sheep" by spreading the teachings of Jesus and nurturing believers on the path of spiritual growth.[5]

Leaving old waters, the disciples embrace their renewed purpose—redemption and restoration empowering them to carry hope's flame forward.

TODAY

It is tempting to characterize the post-Easter story with a triumphant tone, but as we peer into the world of the disciples after Jesus' crucifixion and resurrection, we can imagine a much more complex web of unsettled emotions. When Jesus was humiliated and killed by the empire he challenged, many abandoned him, including Peter, who denied knowing him. All of this was certain to create deep wounds of shame in Peter and the other disciples. So they needed more than just the power of resurrection to heal them from the trauma they had experienced; they needed a whole relational restoration with Jesus. They needed Jesus to reinterpret their past mistakes and failures into something redeeming and healing.

[5] John 21:15-17

Much like the disciples, there will come a time when we come face to face with our need for this form of restoration. We may be confronted with the loss of a loved one, the rupturing of our intimate relationships, or deep personal challenges. We might find ourselves in a position similar to Peter's, denying a truth in our own lives or choosing to be inauthentic to avoid being singled out or associated with the "wrong" people. Perhaps we have been so crippled by a past mistake that we have stopped taking risks that could help us grow. This story poses a question for us: what can give us hope for healing and restoration when everything seems to have gone so wrong?

This passage offers affirmation that Jesus has a different path in mind for us than we might have for ourselves. The hope we need doesn't come in an abstract form—it comes in the person of Jesus. Like with Peter, Jesus does not deal with our histories and failures by ignoring them or leaving them untended. He does not allow our greatest inadequacies or fears to have only one interpretation. Instead, he reinterprets these very symbols and breathes healing and new meaning into them. This is grace.

This new meaning declares that even when we have foreclosed on our future due to our past, we can begin again. It proclaims that when we are disheartened by our failures, we can begin to trust ourselves again. The grace that unfolds over the charcoal fire helps us rebuild our confidence. Not because we will always get it right or because our intuition is perfect, but because we know Jesus is there to heal and restore us through his grace. In the midst of all that we feel and experience, there is grace, there is grace, there is grace.

Abstraction Based on Flower Forms, IV
DAVID KAKABADZÉ, 1921   **WATERCOLOR AND SALT ON PAPER**

Reflect

PAUSE

Sit up straight.

Take a deep breath.

Using the art element (on the previous page),
take a moment to reflect on the story.

PONDER

Invite God to speak to you:

I.

How can we trust in our own ability to start anew
despite our past failures or mistakes?

II.

In what ways can we support others in their paths
towards holistic healing and growth?

II.

How can we seek God to aid us in our own journeys of healing and restoration and in our communities' journeys?

PRAY

God of Grace,
when we feel lost or wounded,
and pain overwhelms us,
may your grace unfold,
and may your love overflow.
Amen.

God's Power

Elijah

God's Power

The Story of Elijah

SYNOPSIS

During a time of disobedience and suffering throughout Israel, the prophet Elijah proves God's strength and power over all other gods.

GOD'S POWER

KEY MOMENT:	FULL READINGS:
1 Kings 18:16-46	1 Kings 16:29-34, 17–18

Read

We meet Elijah for the first time in Israel under the rule of a wicked king named Ahab. Ahab has destroyed the altar of God and instead serves and worships Ba'al, a god of fertility and weather. To Ahab, God is weak and inadequate, and he believes that Ba'al is the one who will ensure his land remains fertile and wealthy. But God is ready to prove otherwise: God instructs Elijah to go to Ahab and tell him there will be a severe drought throughout his land for many years.

So, Elijah goes to Ahab, and the drought comes just as he proclaims.[1] Grasses wither and streams run dry. The land becomes barren and the people of Israel begin to suffer. Months turn to years; the plight becomes worse and worse until, finally, in the third year of the drought, God instructs Elijah to go back to Ahab and tell him that God will send rain back to the land.[2]

When they meet, Elijah rebukes Ahab—how dare he believe Ba'al is more powerful than God! In Ahab's circle, there are now over 450 prophets serving Ba'al. Elijah is appalled that Ahab, the most powerful man in Israel, has coerced a large group of people to follow his god. In his dismay, Elijah sets up a very public situation to prove God's strength and power over Ba'al, in front of everyone.

Elijah instructs Ahab to gather his prophets of Ba'al on Mount Carmel. There, he presents two bulls for sacrifice and tells the prophets of Ba'al to take one of the bulls, create an altar, and call upon their god to light it on fire.[3] For hours on end, the prophets plead for Ba'al to answer, but their god does not respond nor pay attention.

As evening approaches, the prophets grow weary and Elijah tells them to gather around him. He takes twelve stones, one for each of the tribes descended from Jacob, and repairs the altar of God. He prepares the bull for sacrifice and tells the people to pour water three times over the offering and wood. Then, Elijah earnestly prays for God's power to become evident to prove His might over Ba'al to the people.[4]

Suddenly, a fire ignites—burning up the bull, the wood, the stones, and the water! Everything is consumed by flame. The prophets of Ba'al fall to their knees crying out that the Lord is indeed God.

Elijah commands the prophets to be seized and has them killed. He then goes to Ahab and tells him to leave, eat, and drink—for rain will come. Ahab leaves, and Elijah climbs to the top of the mountain, praying for rain. Six times, Elijah's servant claims there is no rain in sight. Finally, on the seventh time, the servant comes and says a tiny cloud the size of man's hand is approaching from the sea.[5] Clouds swell, winds rise, and heavy rains fall upon the barren dry earth, making the land lush and fertile once more.

TODAY

We all have Ahab's in our lives—powerful people, advertisements, and cultural messages—who try to convince us to serve and worship a "Ba'al." We are told to center our lives around money and material objects, or to prioritize status and success. We are told to give all our identity to our physical appearance or personal intellect. In all of these things, we are left with a choice: to be tempted to follow the messages of Ba'al or to listen to the prophets trying to challenge them.

[4] 1 Kings 18:30-38 / [5] 1 Kings 18:41-45

GOD'S POWER

Eventually, these objects will inevitably fail us. We may try to make money and material objects the center of our security, but still feel a lack of safety. We may try to glorify status or success, but there will always be new ladders to climb, eluding goals to chase, and unmet expectations to live up to. We may try to give all our attention to our physical appearance or intellect, but there will always be situations that make us feel ugly or unintelligent. Similar to the prophets of Ba'al's ultimate demise, choosing to worship these things leads to a certain kind of death: our souls left untethered and unsatisfied as we miss out on the full kind of life God wants for us.

Underneath the surface, when we try to serve and worship these things, we are questioning if God is truly more *powerful* than those things. We are wrestling with whether everlasting provision, sustenance, and care truly come from God.

And yet, despite our best efforts to prove otherwise, we all have moments in our lives when the things we try to choose over God fall short, but God remains steadfast and strong. Just like God proved His power over the weather—something Ba'al was supposed to be a god over—time and time again, God proves power over all other objects we try to worship. When we try to make money our security, God proves a better guardian. When we try to make status and success our sense of satisfaction, God proves we are already enough. When we try to place too much emphasis on our own physical appearance or intellect, God proves who we are is already beautiful—inside and out.

In all, God is powerful, and God is ready to show it. May we open our eyes to see.

Nubes en la Sierra
WALTER DE NAVAZIO, 1915

OIL ON CANVAS

Reflect

PAUSE

Sit up straight.

Take a deep breath.

Using the art element (on the previous page), take a moment to reflect on the story.

PONDER

Invite God to speak to you:

I.

Who or what are the "Ba'als" in your life that try to convince you they are more powerful than God?

II.

How have you seen God's power and provision in your life when you have chosen to serve and worship God instead of other things?

PRAY

God of Power,
help us resist
the Ba'als in our midst.
May we see through
false worship's allure,
and choose You
as our true savior.
Amen.

Huldah
& Josiah

The Story of Huldah & Josiah

SYNOPSIS

Prophetess Huldah is entrusted with interpreting a long-lost divine scroll for King Josiah and his entire kingdom. Amidst uncertainty, she guides them towards a greater destiny, away from idolatry and injustice.

KEY MOMENT:	FULL READING:
2 Kings 22:14-20	2 Kings 22–23:30

Read

King Josiah's temple building reform begins, and under the rubble a scroll lies uncovered.[1] Filled with divine laws and commandments, its words serve as a powerful reminder of the covenant between God and God's people. Though faint and distant, these words resonate deeply within the king's heart, stirring the embers of long-forgotten memories and revealing the extent of his kingdom's idolatry—a misguided devotion to fleeting desires and false gods.

Overcome with grief, Josiah tears his robe, trembling under the weight of responsibility he bears for his kingdom's idolatrous inhabitants.[2] Who were these kings in the past, to have allowed idolatry and injustice to spread like a plague throughout the land?

The kingdom was teetering.

With the scroll's Deuteronomic warnings of blessings and curses, Josiah sees a flicker of hope—a chance to guide his nation back to God. He sends his council to Huldah—a respected court prophetess—as a way to ensure the scroll's legitimacy.[3]

As the council beseeches Huldah—their voices laced with urgency—she listens intently, drawing upon the present circumstances. For many years, as a prophet, her responsibility has been to chart a path forward and guide the people toward truth, with the trust that her message will be carried through the spirit of God. "What is the Lord's will for Israel concerning this scroll?" they ask the wise court prophetess. Huldah senses the gravity of the moment. With weighty intention, she speaks, "The burning of incense to other gods has incited Yahweh's burning anger." A heavy burden settles upon her heart, as well as theirs. For they know that her words are an affirmation of God's character. If only her people would choose righteousness over ruin!

Yet, Huldah observes a striking aspect in the unfolding events: God's light shining brightly upon Josiah's governance and reign—his humble, devoted approach to understanding God's buried laws. This is a stark contrast to kings before—Amon and Manessah—who rejected God and filled Jerusalem with innocent blood "from end to end."[4]

The situation is clear to the Prophetess. "Take with you this message," she says, her voice firm yet compassionate. "The Lord has seen you, Josiah. He has heard your cries of repentance for the sins of your people and the kings before you. He will protect you from seeing their demise as a reward for your faith."[5]

With Huldah's words in mind, Israel stands at a precipice of destiny—their path filled with possibility.

TODAY

In Huldah's time, prophecy and the ability to navigate uncertainty were essential skills for a society on the brink of chaos. As a prophet, Huldah's role was to communicate God's will, speaking truth to power and offering guidance in turbulent times. Theologian Dr. Cornel West describes this methodology as "forthtelling"—as opposed to foretelling—as he emphasizes in his work about the importance of addressing current challenges with moral clarity, spiritual wisdom, and a commitment to justice. It is less future-predicting, and more looking at the world around us, *seeing* as God sees.

[4] 2 Kings 21:16 / [5] 2 Kings 22:18-20

In this story, Huldah epitomizes forthtelling prophecy by interpreting the scroll's contents and urging her people to turn away from their ongoing idolatrous ways. Her words serve as a mirror, illuminating Israel's actions in the context of God's divine principles.

How would we respond to the notion of forthtelling in our lives? In a turbulent world, truth-telling may leave us feeling particularly exposed—unveiling our deepest fears and anxieties. Our idolatries—misguided devotion to fleeting desires—become more apparent. When faced with the discovery of the forgotten divine laws, King Josiah could have chosen to ignore or deny their existence. Instead, he humbly sought confirmation from Huldah to course-correct his kingdom's trajectory.

For us today, forthtelling spurs us to tackle urgent issues, dive into tough conversations, and expose ethical and moral concerns that affect our communities. It embodies the spirit of Huldah, inspiring change and leading our world towards a better future.

Seeing the world as God sees provides us hope. In today's fast-paced and complex society, we face numerous uncertainties—from career choices and relationships to societal shifts and technological advancements. Countless injustices such as racism, sexism, environmental decay, plague our society, urgently calling for our attention and action. Our world needs "forthtellers"—those who, like Huldah, respond to our most pressing issues with discernment, humility, and an honest mirror.

The Bible shows us again and again that for change to occur, we must turn back to God and identify the ways in which we ourselves have wavered. There is a hopeful reward for repentance and faithfully speaking the truth in love. May we be curious and open.

Tidal
JONATHAN TODRYK, 2023

OIL, PIGMENT, COFFEE,
AND GESSO ON CANVAS

Reflect

PAUSE

Sit up straight.

Take a deep breath.

Using the art element (on the previous page),
take a moment to reflect on the story.

PONDER

Invite God to speak to you:

I.

As we face challenging truths, how can we adopt
King Josiah's humility and openness to change?

II.

Similar to Huldah—what approaches can we adopt
to practice "forthtelling"? How can we address
pressing issues and promote justice?

III.

What are modern idolatries in our world and how
can we confront them collectively?

PRAY

God, help us see clearly.
In a world filled with confusion
may we be open
and humble.
May we choose
righteousness over ruin.
Amen.

Silence Amidst Grief

Job

The Story of Job

SYNOPSIS

Job, a prosperous man, suffers a sudden immense loss. While friends use aimless words to console his grief, God compassionately shows him the power of silence and stillness.

KEY MOMENT:	FULL READINGS:
Job 42	Job 1–2, 42

Read

OUTLINE

All in one day and seemingly out of nowhere, Job's servants come one after another to deliver news of loss. Until now, Job had been the wealthiest man in the region, but on this day, almost all of his livestock and servants are stolen or killed, and all of his children die in a building collapse.[1]

Job is devastated, but he still praises God.

He is then afflicted with painful boils all over his body.[2] Physical pain joins the emotional pain. Yet, even now, Job wants to remain faithful. He accepts from God both the good and the bad.

Three of Job's friends hear what has happened and make the journey to visit him.[3] They see him from a ways off and wail in deep grief. Job is barely recognizable, his body ravaged by sores. After they arrive, for seven days, all they can do is sit in sheer silence. Each of them is overcome by the presence of such incredible loss and devastation.

But eventually, they grow uncomfortable with the silence, so they fill it with words of explanation. They talk. And talk. And talk some more. Job listens as his friends offer reasons why all of these horrible things have happened to him. They grasp for some sense of meaning amid all of the pain and confusion. Their initial space of silent solidarity becomes filled with words of blame and justification.

Their words anger and hurt Job, and throughout the conversation he defends himself, contending that he is a righteous man and has not displeased God. As

SILENCE AMIDST GRIEF

the waterfall of words flows on, Job receives no benefit. He is not comforted. He does not feel supported. Instead, grows even more defensive, and increasingly eager to prove his integrity.

After many hours of talking, another man arrives to say even more. More explanations, more accusations, more advice, more theologizing. More words. None of this brings back what Job has lost, none of it consoles him, and none of it draws him closer to God.

Finally, in a profound moment, God speaks. But God doesn't offer an explanation for Job's suffering.[4] God doesn't respond to their grief and confusion with more words of blame and accusation or by helping them understand why it happened.

Instead, out of a fierce whirlwind, God asks Job to answer question after question about the vast happenings of creation. He highlights everything from when the wild goats give birth, to how the stars move, to the enormous power of giant creatures in the sea. God asks if Job attends to this diverse expanse of life, a vast world that is moving and changing in every moment. In this way, God emphasizes that He is the one who sees, holds, nurtures, and empowers the incredible expanse of all that is. In this, Job discovers the wisdom of God, and it brings him to silence.

God then restores the possessions that Job has lost and doubles the amount of what he had before.[5] Job's wife gives birth to another seven sons and three daughters, and they have many grandchildren. He lives a long life and dies content at his last breath.

[4] Job 38:1-3   /   [5] Job 42:10-17

TODAY

When someone is grieving, well-intentioned friends can be quick with words of judgment or simplistic explanations. Sometimes, we even say these things to ourselves. This can inadvertently make already significant pain feel even worse.

Being silent and letting ourselves take in the reality of the loss can be difficult. We might avoid silence because in it, we are faced with our sadness or confronted with fears of unpredictable tragedy.

But in Job, God invites us to embrace silence.

It isn't an empty silence, though. God calls Job to turn his attention to the immensity of the natural world, demonstrating God's own vastness as the Creator—to remember that God is the one who holds the wild, expansive world in loving attention. God's immeasurable power and wisdom deeply move Job, and his own words of explanation fall flat. For all the ways he leans on his human perspective to understand the mind and ways of God, he sits in repentance. He sees the limits of words and realizes that in some moments, silence is a more fitting response.

The next time we or someone we love experiences the grief of loss, we are invited to resist the urge to interpret or explain the situation. While being present in grief, we can embrace a time of silence and stillness before God. We can find ways to accompany them—cooking a meal, knitting beside them, washing their dishes—without having to use words.

Job shows us the power of silence and simply being with someone in their pain—not letting words and limited perspectives get in the way of our grieving.

From Zadielská dolina
ĽUDOVÍT ČORDÁK, 1930–1935   INK AND COLOR ON PAPER

Reflect

PAUSE

Sit up straight.

Take a deep breath.

Using the art element (on the previous page), take a moment to reflect on the story.

PONDER

Invite God to speak to you:

I.

How can we resist the urge to explain away someone's grief and simply be present with them?

II.

In what ways can silence and stillness before God be a fitting response to pain and confusion?

III.

What does Job's experience reveal about the limitations of human perspective and the power of God's wisdom?

PRAY

Almighty God,
we pause and listen
for your wisdom.
May we be present
in all grief
and be still before You.
Help us see your power
extend where we cannot reach.
Amen.

Dreams

Joseph

The Story of Joseph

SYNOPSIS

Joseph—a favored son with an unusual talent for dreaming—is sold into slavery by his jealous brothers, only to rise to power in Egypt.

KEY MOMENT:	**FULL READINGS:**
Genesis 39	Genesis 37; 39-41

Read

Joseph is Jacob's twelfth child. Being one of the youngest children, the eleventh son holds no special legal privileges like the first-born; many would have expected Joseph to be given less attention in his household. However, because Joseph is Jacob's first son by his wife Rachel, Jacob favors Joseph—and his half-brothers don't like that very much.[1]

Not only that, Joseph begins to have incredible dreams at a young age. At first, it's a dream of him and his brothers tying up bundles of grain. Suddenly, Joseph's bundle stands up, and his brothers' bundles bow down to Joseph's.[2] When he tells his brothers about this dream, it only causes them to dislike him more. Soon, Joseph has another dream. This time, the sun, the moon, and 11 stars bow before Joseph. Understanding it to be an allegory for their family, this time, even Joseph's father scolds him for his arrogant dream.[3] Joseph doesn't fully understand the implications of all of his dreams at this stage of his life—but he does know they are a gift from God, so he holds onto them in his heart and in his mind.

After years of these seemingly boastful dreams, favoritism, and extra gifts, Joseph's brothers reach the end of their rope and plot to get rid of Joseph. Though one brother, Reuben, protested any serious damage, the rest decide to sell him to the Midianites as a slave.[4] He is sold to Potiphar, captain of the Egyptian guard.

At first look, this seems like a major setback to the dreams God gave Joseph. However, he quickly stands out among Potiphar's servants. Potiphar sees that Joseph has favor with God; things just seemed to work

DREAMS

[1] Genesis 37:3 / [2] Genesis 37:5-7 / [3] Genesis 37:9-10 / [4] Genesis 37:28

out for him. As a result, Joseph is put in charge of Potiphar's household and everything Potiphar owns. Soon, however, Potiphar's wife grows infatuated with Joseph and makes advances toward him. When Joseph protests and flees the room, Potiphar's wife grabs his cloak and accuses him of attempting to rape her. Furious, Potiphar throws Joseph into Pharaoh's prison.[5]

Again, this seems like another setback to Joseph's dreams! But once more, Joseph gains favor—even in prison. Joseph is put in charge of the other prisoners. Then, the Pharaoh's cup-bearer and baker, who are thrown into prison with Joseph, begin having dreams themselves. Joseph, familiar with dreams and trusting God to interpret, correctly interprets their dreams. After the cup-bearer is released from prison, Pharaoh himself begins to have weird dreams. Remembering Joseph from the prison, the cup-bearer shares with his experience of Joseph interpreting his dreams with Pharoah.

So Joseph, thrust into slavery and torn from his family because of his dreams, is called out of prison because of his ability to interpret dreams. With God's help, Joseph interprets the Pharaoh's dreams, which warn of famine ahead. Pharaoh, seeing God at work through Joseph, gives Joseph the second highest office in the land, putting him in the place that Joseph had dreamed about in the days of his youth.[6]

TODAY

Looking at Joseph's story, we see a long, winding journey from being one of the youngest in the family to the second highest in all Egypt. Joseph lost his freedom and experienced betrayal, manual labor, and imprison-

[5] Genesis 39:7-20 / [6] Genesis 41:39-41

ment at the hands of people he once trusted. Though so much was taken away from Joseph, one thing they couldn't take away from him was his dreams.

From a young age, Joseph was immersed in the world of dreams. He had a sense of what God might be doing in his life because of them. By the time he lands in prison, he confidently interprets the dreams of others, which suggests that his relationship with dreaming flourished and evolved throughout his life. This was the way God spoke to and through him. These dreams stayed with Joseph and accompanied him, even in his lowest of lows.

Our ability to dream is just one part of our imagination. As humans, God has gifted us with the ability to imagine and see beyond our current circumstances and envision a different, new reality. Our imagination is one of the places we hold our hopes, creativity, and senses of wonder and beauty. At times, we are conscious and in full control of our dreams and imagination. Other times, like when we're sleeping, dreams come to us on their own terms.

Joseph's story reminds us that following our dreams doesn't mean a smooth and straightforward path. His journey was winding and incredibly bumpy, with the lowest of lows. However, our dreams can go anywhere with us when we hold onto them in our minds and hearts. Though we may be tempted to give up or force our dreams to come true, the invitation is to keep showing up like Joseph did, even in the worst circumstances. God may have a plan to bring us through—and we may just end up where we dreamed we'd be since the beginning.

DREAMS

Sunset in Split
MENCI CLEMENT CRNČIĆ, 1930   **OIL ON CANVAS**

Reflect

Sit up straight.

Take a deep breath.

Using the art element (on the previous page),
take a moment to reflect on the story.

PONDER

Invite God to speak to you:

I.

What is your relationship with dreams and imagination? Do you see both of these things as a way to connect with God?

II.

How can we continue to hold on to our dreams and hopes in the face of adversity and setbacks?

III.

How can dreams inspire with practical action to bring about positive change in our lives?

PRAY

God of Imagination,
thank you for holding visions
for our lives.
May we trust your plan,
to bring us where we dreamed.
Even when life is difficult,
may we hold onto them
each new day.
Amen.

DREAMS

Martha & Mary

The Story of Martha & Mary

SYNOPSIS

As two sisters, Martha and Mary, warmly welcome Jesus into their home, each discovers and wrestles with their own unique way of honoring their esteemed guest.

KEY MOMENT:	FULL READING:
Luke 10:38-42	Luke 10

Read

OUTLINE

As Jesus travels through an unknown village, he is welcomed by Martha into her and Mary's home.[1] As a person who takes pride in her hospitality, Martha is honored to host Jesus and his disciples. But, as any good host knows, it takes a lot of work—including tasks like cleaning the house, preparing large amounts of food, and making sure everyone is comfortable.

Martha knows the work will be cumbersome, but she has a younger sister, Mary, who will help—or so she thinks. As she struggles to handle all of the preparations, Mary is seated at the feet of Jesus, listening to his wisdom.[2] One can only imagine the frustration Martha is feeling. Here she is, trying to make everything perfect for their guest, while Mary is simply sitting down, listening to stories instead of helping her. As the older sister, she understands her responsibility in taking care of such things and expects her younger sister to help. Does Jesus not see this? Does he not care about the efforts she is making to be a good host? Surely he must understand.

While Martha continues her work, silently fuming, Mary sits listening intently to every word Jesus says. Yes, she could be helping her sister, but how often does she get to sit at the feet of our Lord and hear his divine wisdom? As this opportunity is mostly only given to disciples (and primarily men), Mary is not going to give up this rare chance willingly. Martha will surely understand, right?

As if on cue, Martha turns to Jesus and says, "Do you not care that Mary has left me to do the work by myself?! Tell her to help me!"[3]

HONORING WORSHIP AND SERVICE

The room goes silent as everyone turns their attention to Martha and then to Mary. Mary, embarrassed, lowers her eyes. Maybe she doesn't know her place after all. Maybe her place at Jesus' feet is a mistake, and she is only granted access because no one noticed her. Now that she is exposed, surely she will be rejected. Who does she think she is anyways?

But Jesus turns lovingly to Martha. "Martha, Martha," he says, stating her name twice to show his endearment to her. "You are distracted by many things, but only a few things are needed, even only one thing. Mary has chosen her place. It is the better choice, and it will not be taken from her."[4]

TODAY

Despite its use, this passage isn't about pitting one sister's actions over another. Martha's cry isn't about an antagonistic relationship between her and her sister but instead about wanting to feel seen in her efforts. Both sisters made the choice to honor Jesus in their own way. Jesus' words to Martha are not a rebuke of her acts of service. Instead, he gently reminds her that there is more to life than tasks. He came to her home not because she would have the best food or provisions, but so he could spend time with her. Mary chose the "better choice" not because their choices are based on a hierarchy of value, but because Jesus wanted to spend time with them.

"It is the better choice" is a phrase that has been used to antagonize overachievers since those words were first spoken. It is often said in our communities, "doing tasks is not important; what is important is to sit at the feet of Jesus." Filled with shame, the Marthas of the world often shy away from tasks, feeling as if their gifts of service are lesser. Likewise, those who identify with Mary are often placed on a pedestal, treated as if they are examples of true faithfulness, and used as fodder for the shame thrown at their siblings.

Things are not so black and white, however. There are many gifts we can offer to God and our community. Like Mary, we can offer our attention, and our worship by sitting at the feet of Jesus. But like Martha, we can also offer our service, hospitality, and care. This is not an either/or situation, it is a both/and one. Like these two sisters, we have the capacity to honor God in our worship and service.

This story resonates with another pair of siblings in the Bible: the prodigal son and his older brother.[5] Both the older brother and Martha took pride in their commitments and loyalties, doing what was asked of them. Similarly, both younger siblings made unconventional choices, leading them down different paths marked by humility. Like Jesus' response to Martha, the father's response to the older brother honors the work and commitment he made. However, it also gently reminds him that more than one path is possible and that even unconventional choices, when they lead you back to the feet of your beloved, should be honored and celebrated. Although these are not the only tales of older and younger siblings in the Bible, these two stories remind us of the many ways we can honor God.

[5] Luke 15:11-32

Forest (Morning Sun)

JOHANN WALTER-KURAU, 1904   **OIL ON CANVAS**

Reflect

PAUSE

Sit up straight.

Take a deep breath.

Using the art element (on the previous page), take a moment to reflect on the story.

PONDER

Invite God to speak to you:

I.

Do you see serving others and spending time with God as mutually exclusive? What does balancing their importance look like?

II.

Have you ever felt unappreciated or unseen? How can you remind yourself that your efforts are valued by God and your community?

III.

How can we embrace unconventional paths when it comes to our lives of faith?

PRAY

God,
thank you for seeing me
and loving me as I am.
May I remember:
there is nothing I have to do
to earn your love.
Being present with you
is enough.
Amen.

Mary

The Story of Mary

REVOLUTION

SYNOPSIS

Mary's visit to her cousin Elizabeth leads her to sing a powerful song of hope and resistance against oppression, as they anticipate the fulfillment of God's promises.

KEY MOMENT:	**FULL READING:**
Luke 1:39-56	Luke 1:1-56

Read

OUTLINE

When the angel Gabriel tells Mary she is pregnant, and that her much older cousin Elizabeth is also pregnant, Mary knows she needs to go visit her relative as soon as possible.[1]

After Mary greets Elizabeth and they share all their exciting news, Mary starts to feel even more energized.[2] Gabriel's news was shocking to her, and after talking it through with Elizabeth, she is convinced that God has plans for something even bigger. She knows that it is a miracle for both of them to be pregnant—and she feels that God is near; she senses something shifting. Both women see how God is moving into their day-to-day, personal lives and believe God must also be planning a rescue for their entire oppressed community.

Mary can hardly control herself. A rallying cry is on her lips. Instead of telling Elizabeth what she's feeling, she is compelled to sing.[3] She draws upon the sacred texts she has memorized since she was little. She has read the Psalms of Israel and can recite God's promises forwards and backwards.

One of those promises is that her people will not be oppressed forever. Rome is cruel to the Jewish people, her people. But she understands the promises of God and knows a rescue and a reset is going to happen—and that she is about to be a critical part of the story. She senses the birth of her son means a power dynamic will flip. The words spill out of her through this powerful rebuke of corruption. She begins to chant and sing, with her hands in the air. She sings about rich people being sent away, hungry people being fed, rulers being taken off their thrones, and the lowly poor people being raised up. Mary sings

[1] Luke 1:26-28 / [2] Luke 1:39-41 / [3] Luke 1:46-56 MSG

about power dynamics being flipped because Rome is rich and God's people are suffering. She sees the turmoil every day, but she understands the promises God made to her people—and she believes God. She believes so much that she is not afraid to call out corruption and the unfair oppression of her people in the form of a melody.

After Mary sings the triumphant song in front of her cousin, they start to prepare the house for Mary's extended stay. Energized by one another—and with little humans starting to grow inside of them—they know a season of rest and preparation is needed. They spend three months together anticipating a season of God's promises being fulfilled.[4]

This is a bold side of Mary that we don't often hear about. Her strong prophetic words are a gift to us today, and are still applicable. She believed God's promises and shows us what radical faith looks like. One of the promises she believed is that God will bring justice and rescue the poor.

Mary knew how much these practical, societal changes were needed because she was living in this story, not from a position of power, but from a lowly position. These are not abstract emotional experiences. Mary is singing about things that are happening to people's bodies. She has in mind the Romans and the way her people have suffered under their rule. She is giving voice to the steadfast hope of the Jewish people—they did not believe they would be oppressed forever. She is taking God's magnifying glass, holding it over people who are forgotten, and telling them, "You're about to be seen, fed, and loved."

[4]Luke 1:56

Dietrich Bonhoeffer, a German pastor and theologian who was executed by the Nazis during WWII, called Mary's song in Luke 1 "the most passionate, the wildest, one might even say the most revolutionary hymn ever sung." What does that revolution look like for us today? We have the opportunity to be honest about our own starvation and poverty; this covenant song from Mary can be for us too. God wants to meet us in our present needs, starting with our physical needs: in a society that has normalized people, even children, sleeping on the streets and in the cold, God wants to meet us in shaping a new, tangible world where everyone's physical needs are satisfied.

And, even if we might not physically be in the mud and need to be pulled out, mentally, it can often feel like we are trudging our way through life—with experiences of loneliness, desperation, depression, and grief. Hopelessness is an oppressor that people need rescuing from as well. In these needs, too, God wants to show us a new path.

Mary repeated the promises of God out loud in community with Elizabeth, and it sustained her. Often, the promises of God are fulfilled by the people around us who show up and support us—physically, spiritually, mentally, emotionally—as we continue to cling to hope. This, in turn, can help us inspire revolution in others—helping them take their own next steps towards healing and bring forth justice in their own communities. In every season, we are invited to follow Mary into a revolutionary liberation. We get to participate in the coming of Jesus and the shaping of a new world by remembering that God cares for the poor and oppressed *in all ways*. Mary's cry for justice reminds us we can be a part of keeping God's promises alive today.

Five Cloud Horizon
BRYAN YE-CHUNG, 2022

OIL ON CANVAS

Reflect

PAUSE

Sit up straight.

Take a deep breath.

Using the art element (on the previous page),
take a moment to reflect on the story.

PONDER

Invite God to speak to you:

I.

Where do you long for change, both internally and
externally, mentally and physically?

II.

In our communities, how can we draw upon the
promises of God to sustain us in times of difficulty?

III.

How can we participate with God in shaping a new
world where the last are first?

PRAY

Dear God,
lead us to revolution.
Where the poor are fed,
the mighty
no longer oppress,
and the first are last.
Guide us
to keep your promises
alive.
Amen.

Learning / Growing / Transformation

Nicodemus

The Story of Nicodemus

SYNOPSIS

Nicodemus, a religious scholar, encounters Jesus and is challenged to rethink his beliefs—leading him on a journey of growth and learning that ultimately transforms him.

KEY MOMENT:	FULL READING:
John 3:1-21	John 7:45-52, 19:38-42

Read

A flame softly flickers late into the night as Nicodemus studies the ancient scrolls with a keen mind and nimble fingers. Seeking to interpret the divine law for his people, Nicodemus finds deep purpose in his esteemed role as a reputable Jewish scholar and Pharisee.

But in this wondrous night something changes for Nicodemus. He encounters Jesus. And suddenly, the man who is supposed to have all the answers finds himself asking questions—questions about the teaching and works of the one reputed to possess miraculous powers; the one who possibly might be the long-awaited Messiah.[1]

Away from the crowds, under the cover of night, he seeks an honest but cautious audience with Jesus. Unlike many of his colleagues, Nicodemus is slower to jump to conclusions about the character and intent of this newly arrived and increasingly popular rabbi.[2] He affirms that all signs point to Jesus being sent by God "to teach us." His posture is one of curiosity towards learning something new. However, Nicodemus' openness is immediately put to the test when Jesus offers less of an answer, but more of an invitation to transform himself—to be "born again."[3]

Nicodemus is confused by the mechanics of such an overture. Biologically, it makes no sense.[4] How could a person be born *again*? There is no turning back the clock. What we become is what we are. As Jesus tries to move Nicodemus away from his literal interpretation of what has been shared, he speaks of a rebirth, a transformation that is purely and wholly the work of God—of the Spirit in and through us.[5] For a learned man whose counsel has been based on living by following divine laws, the implication of life being a gift *received* rather than *achieved* is confusing.

Still uncertain, Nicodemus exits the scene, having shown no indication of greater comprehension. Seemingly, he departs as a perplexed character from the Gospel of John with more questions than answers.

This is, however, not the end of Nicodemus' journey of faith. Much later on in the Gospel of John, we realize Jesus' remarks have made an impression on Nicodemus. He has been slowly ruminating on Jesus' words and gradually feeling a deeper connection to his teachings; the text never clarifies if Nicodemus ever understands Jesus wholly or perfectly, but regardless Nicodemus is eventually spurred into action. When his fellow Pharisees try unsuccessfully to have Jesus arrested, it is Nicodemus who stands alone, who stands apart in reminding them even the Law of God declares a person is innocent until proven guilty.[6]

Even after his counsel to his colleagues goes unheeded and Jesus is put to death, it is Nicodemus who boldly comes forward to ensure Jesus is buried with dignity and honor.[7] When everyone else has run for cover, Nicodemus breaks ranks with the rest of the Jewish leadership and risks expulsion from the community, the life he has always known. His doubts and his questions may still remain. And yet, no longer under the cover of darkness but in the light of day, as Nicodemus lovingly tends to Jesus' body, he puts his life in Christ's hands. By faith, his rebirth, his transformation by God has only just begun.

[6] John 7:45-52 / [7] John 19:38-42

LEARNING / GROWING / TRANSFORMATION

We live in a fast-paced world. We try to keep up with its pace, but we look around and it seems like everyone else is figuring things out and progressing faster than we are. The pressure only grows when we feel like we are running behind. We are weighed down by the fear of arriving too late, of missing out on life's good things.

Such urgency and anxiety can also mark our journey of faith. We find ourselves surrounded by others who are so certain and earnest in their beliefs, even as we continue to have questions and doubts. Our indecision and hesitation in taking action can be framed as leaving us left behind.

Nicodemus' story encourages us to refrain from passing such judgments—to ourselves or to others. At first glance, we might assume that Nicodemus was unable to understand Jesus' words. The story cuts away without us knowing how he responded to this teaching. We do know that he doesn't continue to follow Jesus in that moment, as he is numbered among the Jewish leaders in John 7. But just because he didn't leave everything and begin to follow Jesus immediately, doesn't mean that Jesus' words weren't working in him. His process doesn't keep him from getting to the point of trusting Jesus. It's just that—a process. Divine change—growth and maturity—was happening little by little.

Thankfully, "late" is not a concept known to God. As the Creator and Master of all time, there's never too late with God. Even when we feel like we are falling behind, Jesus meets us where we are and as we are. Through our questions, through our doubts, the Spirit leads us forward, continually refining and shaping us into becoming the best version of ourselves in Christ.

LEARNING / GROWING / TRANSFORMATION

The Narrows
JACKIE TAM, 2021   **DIGITAL**

Reflect

PAUSE

Sit up straight.

Take a deep breath.

Using the art element (on the previous page),
take a moment to reflect on the story.

PONDER

Invite God to speak to you:

I.

How can we stay receptive to Jesus' transformative
power amid uncertainty and doubt?

II.

What practices can help us develop patience for
ourselves and others, recognizing that personal
growth is an ongoing process?

III.

How can we learn to see the journey, rather than
the destination, as the most important thing in
our relationship with God?

PRAY

God, help us see
the journey You have for us.
One step at a time,
with You as our guide.
We trust your process
to shape and refine us.
Show us who we were made to be.
Amen.

LEARNING / GROWING / TRANSFORMATION

Courage / Boldness

Paul

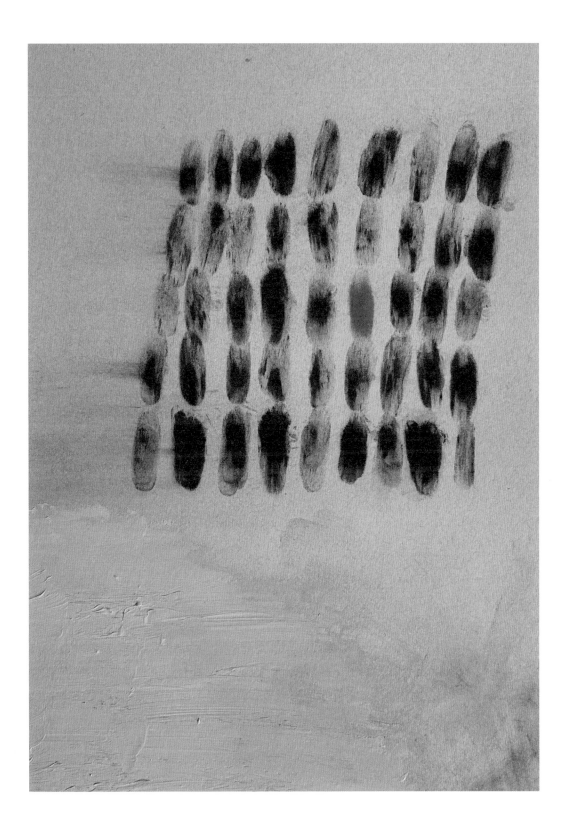

The Story of Paul

SYNOPSIS

Amidst a raging storm at sea, Paul is a beacon of courage for his whole ship. His unwavering confidence in God's plan for his life empowers him to inspire others.

KEY MOMENT:	KEY MOMENT:
Acts 27:13-44	Acts 26–28

Read

OUTLINE

The sky is beautiful. A gentle south wind fills the sails. The blue waters of the Mediterranean Sea look like a field of sapphires. The ship's bow cuts through the waves like a needle through fine cloth.[1]

Suddenly, a gale jerks the ship. Menacing gray clouds roll in faster than a Roman chariot. The once crystal waters now froth with white peaks at every swell. It is now the waves that threaten to cut through the boat. The storm ravages the ship so violently that the sailors pass ropes around the hull in attempts to keep it together. The whole ship feels like it's bursting at the seams.[2]

The passengers on the boat are prisoners and Roman guards: hardened criminals or trained military personnel. Even they are quaking, praying to whatever pantheon of gods they ascribe to. Even the sailors are panicking as they throw cargo overboard to keep the ship afloat.

The storm lasts days. Neither the sun nor the moon have shown themselves, as if they too are afraid of this tempest. Anxiety. Fear. Hopelessness.

Amidst the chaos of the sea and the soul, one man stands up: Paul of Tarsus. He is an anomaly amongst the prisoners. Though he had committed no act of violent crime, he has been accused as an anarchist because of his association with Jesus. The only reason that he sailed on this boat was because he had made an appeal to Caesar. For some reason, he chose to remain in this bureaucratic judicial system and bring his case to the highest court in the land.

Paul opens his mouth. "I urge you to keep up your courage, because not one of you will be lost; only the

COURAGE / BOLDNESS

[1] Acts 27:1-8 / [2] Acts 27:13-20   **163**

ship will be destroyed." His voice booms with confidence, somehow rising louder than the howling winds. Where does this courage come from? He is not a sailor or a soldier. He knows nothing of the seas.

"Last night an angel of the God to whom I belong and whom I serve stood beside me and said, 'Do not be afraid, Paul. You must stand trial before Caesar; and God has graciously given you the lives of all who sail with you.' So keep up your courage, men, for I have faith in God that it will happen just as he told me." [3]

Something about Paul's tone compels the passengers and the crew to keep up hope. Perhaps this man, the one prisoner who deserves freedom, does not deserve to perish in the storm. It is not Paul's nautical knowledge, his swimming skill, nor his social standing that gives him courage. Paul has heard God's word from the angel. This message helps him understand his place in God's story. Paul sees this storm as a mere detour on his way to proclaim Jesus to Caesar. And as he focuses on God's grand story, the storm becomes small.

A few days later, Paul encourages them to eat. The storm is nearly over. The Roman officers had never imagined listening to a prisoner, but Paul's boldness compels them.[4] The storm finally breaks. Golden daylight peaks over the horizon. The ship calms and everyone is safe, just as Paul had promised. The sailors and prisoners and soldiers are all left to wonder, who is this God that gave Paul such confidence in the face of death? [5]

TODAY

The stories of courage in our world today are made up of Marvel movies, sports legends, Korean dramas, and CEO successes. These are all people who muster up the confidence to chase what they love. As we consume these stories, we let their voices influence our perception.

[3] Acts 27:22-25 NIV / [4] Acts 27:33-36 / [5] Acts 27:39-44

The source of Biblical courage is quite different. The source of Biblical courage is the story that Jesus is writing in our lives. According to scripture, boldness is understanding how our moments and seasons of trials fit into God's grand narrative. As disciples of Jesus, we are bold not because we love things, but because we are loved.

When we understand God's story and divine plan for our life, we find the unshakeable courage that Paul has. We do this by attentively listening to God's voice as Paul did in the storm. God is always trying to serenade us with beautiful dreams for our lives. As we let God shape our story, we find that we can face every storm with deep confidence.

It is tempting to simply "muster up" courage as if it is some tangible liquid we can draw from a well. Courage is hardly so straightforward. In fact, if we interviewed Paul about where his courage came from, he would start from the beginning of his testimony when he met Jesus. He would continue talking about all the ways that God has been good in his life. Likewise, in order to live courageous lives, we must first hear God's voice in our lives, then tell our stories with God in them. From there, we can discern God's dreams for us. And when we know what God is doing in our lives, how can a storm be scary?

In the end, our courage is not only a gift for us but also a blessing to others. When we live unafraid of the storms of life, it allows the people around us to wonder about our God. It gives them the freedom to ask questions and have hope.

Let us choose to live in God's goodness. When we do, we cannot help but be courageous.

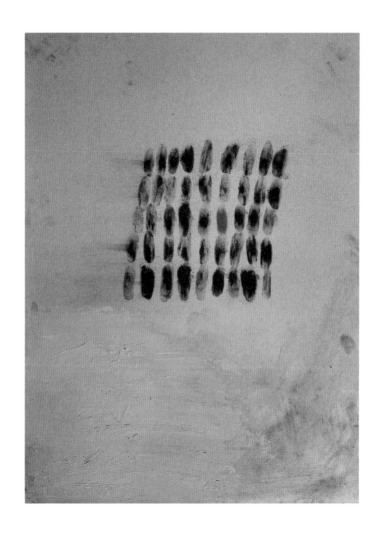

Provision, Protection, Preservation
JONATHAN TODRYK, 2023   **OIL AND PIGMENT ON PAPER**

Reflect

PAUSE

Sit up straight.

Take a deep breath.

Using the art element (on the previous page),
take a moment to reflect on the story.

PONDER

Invite God to speak to you:

I.

What are some ongoing "storms" in our world?
What does it look like to be a beacon of courage
for those around you?

II.

How does understanding God's character give us
courage amidst adversity?

III.

What are some practical ways we can actively
exercise listening to God's voice and deepen our
understanding of God's story in our lives?

PRAY

God, I confess
my fear of the storm.
When chaos stirs
in the world around me,
show me the story
you have for my life,
so that I may have courage.
Amen.

Priscilla & Aquila

The Story of Priscilla & Aquila

SYNOPSIS

Despite many concerns, Priscilla and Aquila offer their home to host various church members on their unexpected travels.

KEY MOMENT:	FULL READING:
Acts 18:18-28	Acts 18

Read

Priscilla and her husband Aquila never intended to make their home in Corinth. But when Emperor Claudius deports all Jews from Rome, Priscilla and Aquila, being Jewish-Christians, find themselves homeless; they move to Corinth out of necessity.

As they build a new life there, they cross paths with the famed Apostle Paul. When Paul later visits their house, Priscilla and Aquila learn that Paul not only shares their faith in Jesus, but he is also in the same line of work as a tentmaker.[1] Priscilla and Aquila offer to host Paul so he can continue what he has come to Corinth to do: teach about Jesus. It's a risky invitation. At this time, teaching about Jesus in the shadow of the Roman Empire and mainstream Judaism was unsafe. But Paul accepts their invitation, and for nearly two years—despite the potential peril—Priscilla and Aquila choose to provide Paul with a safe home and stable employment as a tentmaker.[2]

When Paul decides to leave Corinth and make his way to Syria, Priscilla and Aquila decide to leave Corinth too. The decision isn't hard; Paul has become like family to them, and Corinth was never their intended home. But when the three stop in Ephesus, Priscilla and Aquila decide to stay there instead.[3] Unlike their move to Corinth, this is their decision. So they say their goodbyes to Paul—but their story doesn't end there.

Continuing to be generous hosts, Priscilla and Aquila decide to once again open their home to others in Ephesus. They host a house church where they serve

GENEROUS HOSTING

as pastors—again risking their personal safety to offer a safe space for their new Christian friends.

One Sabbath, Priscilla and Aquila hear a man named Apollos speaking in the Synagogue. Apollos was a Jew who had heard about Jesus from disciples of John the Baptist and who was excited to share what he knew about this messiah. Priscilla and Aquila invite him into their home, and Apollos, like Paul, accepts their generous invitation. They share with him the full story of Jesus and bring him into the wider Ephesian Christian community.[4] Apollos—filled with wisdom and energized by his gracious hosts—eventually leaves to preach the gospel in Achaia and goes on to become a prominent Christian teacher.

Eventually, Emperor Claudius dies. Priscilla and Aquila, who have been living in Ephesus for quite some time, feel it is time to return home to Rome. There, they continue to be generous hosts for the Christian community in Rome, and use their gifts of hospitality for the Kingdom of God.[5]

TODAY

We only have a small glimpse into Priscilla and Aquila's story, but in the little we have, we're given the remarkable opportunity to see how something as unassuming as hosting a community can be a radical act.

Everywhere they lived, Priscilla and Aquila created a home and shared it with others, even when it came at a cost. Without Priscilla and Aquila's generous hospi-

[4] Acts 18:24-26 / [5] Romans 16:3-5

tality, Paul might not have stayed in Corinth so long, spending week after week reasoning with the other Jews in the Synagogue. Apollos may not have matured into the respected Christian teacher he is known as today. We can only imagine the impact their hospitality must have had on all the other Christians who met in their home to worship—countless stories of people finding safety and community.

The story of Priscilla and Aquila invites us to consider our own relationship with hosting and hospitality. Even if we find ourselves in a place we didn't choose or expect to be, like Priscilla and Aquila did in Corinth, we have an opportunity to use whatever home or space or resource we do have. Instead of focusing on the reasons it might be inconvenient, we can try to see what is possible with an openness like theirs.

It's too easy to make excuses and ignore opportunities in front of us. Life is busy and complicated. People aren't always reliable. But if we're able to shift our perspective to see the possibilities, we might have a unique opportunity to open our lives up to others in a new way. What might happen if we take advantage of an opportunity like this? What will happen if we are consistently open with our life? We never know who we might meet, who we might be able to help, who might help us, and what God might do through us.

Paisaje
WALTER DE NAVAZIO, 19TH CENTURY   OIL ON CANVAS

Reflect

Sit up straight.

Take a deep breath.

Using the art element (on the previous page),
take a moment to reflect on the story.

PONDER

Invite God to speak to you:

I.

In what ways have we experienced the transformative power of hospitality in our lives?

II.

Reflect on a time when someone's hospitality left a lasting impact. How can we emulate their example?

III.

How can we extend generosity and create a safe space for others, even when it may come at a cost?

PRAY

God, help us host
with generosity.
Make our homes
safe spaces.
Like Priscilla and Aquila,
may we take risks for love.
Our homes,
not just ours,
be for all beloved.
Amen.

The Prison Guard

The Story of The Prison Guard

SYNOPSIS

A prison guard, who initially imprisons Paul and Silas, becomes an unexpected companion in salvation.

KEY MOMENT:	FULL READING:
Acts 16:25-34	Acts 16:16-40

Read

Paul and Silas are brought before the authorities in Philippi for causing a disturbance. The disturbance? Paul had rebuked a spirit of divination, or fortune telling, from an enslaved woman. The reason for the authorities' concern is not merely religious disagreement; it is the fact that they had made money off of her fortune telling. Now that this spirit has left her, so too has her enslavers' ability to exploit her for their own financial gain.

Thus, Paul and Silas are handed over to the authorities, subjected to flogging, and ultimately cast into prison. We then meet the prison guard. We don't get a lot of information about him, but what we do know is that he follows the orders given by the magistrates to lock up Paul and Silas. In an effort to ensure they are securely confined, the guard places them in a cell deep in the prison and fastens their feet with chains.[1]

At midnight, Paul and Silas are still awake, praying and singing songs of worship to God. Without warning, a powerful earthquake strikes, shaking the prison. The doors of the prison cells fling open, and the chains come undone. The prison guard is awakened from his sleep by the commotion caused by the earthquake.[2] As the person in charge of the prisoners, he sees that the doors have been opened and believes that he's made a grave mistake. The prisoners have escaped on his watch! Seeing this, and knowing the severe punishment and blame that will fall to him, the guard prepares to take his own life.

But then, a voice calls from within the prison: "Don't hurt yourself! We're still here!"[3] The guard rushes to where the voice came from—it is Paul's voice, and

SALVATION

Silas is still with him. Just as the prison's foundations were shaken by the earthquake, so now the prison guard trembles before the disciples. Only a moment ago, the prison guard was ready to take his own life; instead, he brings Paul and Silas outside and asks them what he must do to be saved. Their answer is simple: put your trust in Jesus.[4]

Paul and Silas share the word of the Lord with the guard and his household. We don't know what passages were recited, what words were spoken, or how Paul and Silas explained the Gospel. What we do know is that whatever they discussed leads to a radical act against the prison itself: the guard washes their wounds from the flogging. In the span of only an evening, this prison guard goes from an agent of the prison to one who washes wounds.

In the wake of these events, the guard and his entire family are baptized. Just as the waters washed over and cleansed the wounds of Paul and Silas, so too are the guard's and his family's spiritual wounds washed in the waters of baptism.

Perhaps most striking, however, is how this brief story ends: they all eat together. The divine disruption of the prison through an earthquake brings those once separated by doors and chains, and power and status, to be gathered at a table together. They feast and rejoice over all that has taken place.

TODAY

If we perceive the prison story only as an example of divine intervention, we might miss the deeper meaning before us. As we explore the narrative, we see

[4] Acts 16:31

a vision of salvation that is wider and more tangible than we are often led to believe. Salvation encompasses a reordering of power and the righting of wrongs.

At face value, the disciples' statement urging the guard to believe in the Lord Jesus in order to be saved can sound like a modern-day evangelist leading a new convert in the "sinner's prayer." However, against the cultural and political backdrop of the time, the statement is as much about believing in Jesus as it is about rejecting allegiance to Caesar's government. This is what makes the prison guard's conversion so radical; it's not simply related to the soul—it's a radical reorientation of his whole life and how he chooses to act within this problematic system.

What can we learn about salvation from this story? Many of us have encountered these narratives in contexts of messages such as "saving our soul to get to heaven"; however, the salvation story here is bigger, broader, and more all-encompassing—it is collectively and physically transformative. As theologian Henri Nouwen says, "The power of salvation lies not only in the promise of an eternal life but in the restoration of our humanity, our relationships, and the world we inhabit."

The prison guard washing Paul and Silas's wounds is part of what salvation truly is—a metamorphosis from animosity to newfound friendship, the shattering of barriers, the creation of empathy, and the literal sharing of a meal. Salvation transforms *everything*—not just our souls, but also the quality of our relationships and the reality of our lives. Through salvation, we are all invited to feast together at the bountiful table of life, here and now.

Pampa
PEDRO FIGARI, 1880-1938   OIL ON CARDBOARD

Reflect

PAUSE

Sit up straight.

Take a deep breath.

Using the art element (on the previous page),
take a moment to reflect on the story.

PONDER

Invite God to speak to you:

I.

In what ways have our own cultural and political
contexts shaped our understanding of salvation?
How can we attain a more profound understanding of it in light of this story?

II.

In what ways can we actively participate in the
physical and transformative nature of salvation
within our own communities?

PRAY

God of Salvation,
we trust in your power,
to transform all things.
May our faith in you
bring newness into our world.
May we wash
the wounds of others,
and share in hope and love,
together.
Amen.

SALVATION

Rahab

The Story of Rahab

SYNOPSIS

In the midst of a conflict between the Israelites and Jericho, Rahab, a marginalized woman, courageously shelters Israelite spies, driven by her unwavering faith in a God who delivers salvation.

KEY MOMENT:	FULL READINGS:
Joshua 2:1-22; 6:23	Joshua 2, 6

Read

OUTLINE

Rahab is a woman doing her best to survive amid desperate circumstances. Although she finds herself in a city named Jericho, which is renowned for being a fortress, Rahab lives in a poor part of town. Her house is positioned on the embankment between the upper and lower city walls—built into Jericho's first line of defense; therefore, it is more exposed and far less secure than the homes in the upper part of the city.[1]

Living in a patriarchal society without a husband or any children, leaves Rahab marginalized and vulnerable. Her means of sustaining a living are limited, and she isn't merely trying to provide for herself. Rahab also carries the burden and responsibility of providing for her father, mother, brothers, and sisters.[2] Faced with few options, she endures by leveraging her role as the mistress of her home. Rahab operates both as an innkeeper—providing food, drink, and a place to sleep for weary travelers—and as a sex worker, offering her body to those willing to pay the price.[3] Her given profession is less of a choice and driven more by crippling economic need.

Rahab remains aware of what is happening beyond her doors. She knows well the story of a growing rival group of people called the Israelites, who are being led by the hand of the Lord God, first out of slavery in Egypt then through the trials of the wilderness, drawing near the border of the Jordan River.[4] One evening, two strangers enter her establishment, and Rahab immediately recognizes them as advance scouts sent from this rival group. And yet surprisingly, when word travels fast about the spies she is housing, Rahab doesn't turn them over to the authorities.[5]

[1] Joshua 2:15 / [2] Joshua 2:12-13 / [3] Joshua 2:1-3 / [4] Joshua 2:10 / [5] Joshua 2:3-5

Instead, defying the orders of the king of the city, she hides them on the flat roof of her house, under large bundles of flax while sending their pursuers on a wild goose chase.[6]

Later that evening, as she speaks further with the two guests she is protecting, Rahab demonstrates that she possesses more than knowledge about them, but also faith in the God they worship. Everyone in Jericho realizes a battle against the Israelites—one in which they will certainly be defeated—is imminent. Yet while the rest of the people, out of their fear, choose to fight a losing battle rather than surrendering, Rahab confesses and yields herself before the Lord's mercy and provision.[7]

Rahab seeks to follow, through her actions, the God she only knew by reputation. Her choice to shelter and protect the Israelite spies is not first conditioned upon her and her family being spared later. Rahab preserves their lives believing the Lord will be gracious to her. Again, this is faith—faith in action.

Rahab continues to walk by faith as she helps the two Israelites escape from the city unharmed. Before leaving, they vow to safeguard Rahab and her family once the fighting begins by means of a visual signal—a scarlet cord—to be hung from the window of her house.[8] This piece of twine serves as a public symbol of her new allegiance. Much like the blood of the lamb that marked the doors of the Israelites' homes in Egypt, which served as a marker of salvation from death and release from slavery, Rahab is about to experience her own personal exodus to freedom.

Rahab's mustard seed of faith leads her beyond surviving the battle of Jericho to becoming a part of the newly formed nation of Israel. As the first recorded Gentile convert, Rahab eventually marries into the esteemed royal tribe of Judah, marrying a man named Salmon. Later she becomes the mother of Boaz, the kinsman-redeemer who married Ruth.[9] Ruth and Boaz's offspring would eventually produce the line of King David, whose lineage ultimately traces all the way to Jesus Christ. And yet, more than for her pivotal place in the genealogy of the Messiah of all creation, Rahab is best remembered for the testimony of her faith—believing, trusting, and relying on the God she had never seen but had only heard about.[10]

  [6] Joshua 2:6, 22 / [7] Joshua 2:11-13 / [8] Joshua 2:14-18 / [9] Matthew 1:5-17 / [10] Hebrews 11:1-2, 31

Maybe we can identify with a sense of being walled in by some impossible circumstance: a toxic and dysfunctional relationship, an all-consuming and uhealthy addiction, a nagging and debilitating illness or injury, or a seemingly insurmountable financial crisis. Like Rahab, we are trying our best to survive. We hear stories of God's deliverance, and yet we struggle to perceive any sign of divine intervention amid our own daily troubles.

If we're honest, what we see happening around us makes it easier to recognize our doubts than it does something or someone in which to believe. Our faith, any semblance of trust in God we can muster, feels more blind than true. We can start to wonder—maybe even fear—if we can manage to have enough faith to keep the walls around us from tumbling down.

What we learn from the story of Rahab is that the power of faith is not about any sense of the conviction we can muster—it is paying attention and yielding before the revelation of God's presence in our lives, often in surprising ways. Having faith is not about comprehending the fullness of who God is and how God works; it is about receiving and acting on the opportunity we are given by God at each step in our journey.

Walking by faith isn't negotiating or bargaining with our Creator to get what we need to survive. Walking by faith is trusting in what God has done in the past and following—rather than fighting—God's lead towards the promise of a future in which we can thrive. We can start by letting go of what we fear and daring to believe in a life beyond the walls we know—a life of possibility and freedom. It is beginning to live into such a future, as Rahab demonstrates, by courageously offering hospitality to strangers, boldly protecting life as it is being threatened, and even defiantly loving our perceived enemies.

Girl With Blonde Hair
HELENE SCHJERFBECK, 1916   **OIL ON CANVAS**

Reflect

PAUSE

Sit up straight.

Take a deep breath.

Using the art element (on the previous page),
take a moment to reflect on the story.

PONDER

Invite God to speak to you:

I.

In what ways do you relate to Rahab's desperate circumstances, and how can her story inspire you to persevere in your own life?

II.

In what areas of our lives do we struggle to see God's intervention? How can we continue to seek God's guidance?

PRAY

God,
When we feel walled in,
and crises compound,
may we hear your voice
and hold to your promises.
Teach us to walk
towards a future
in which we can thrive.
Amen.

Rizpah

The Story of Rizpah

MOURNING FOR JUSTICE

SYNOPSIS

Rizpah is left with few options and little power following the death of her sons. When she publicly mourns their deaths and dishonor, those in power are moved to enact justice.

KEY MOMENT:	FULL READINGS:
2 Samuel 21:10-14	2 Samuel 3:6-11; 21:1-14

Read

We first encounter Rizpah in the midst of a political power struggle between the House of David and the House of Saul. She is a daughter of Aiah and the concubine to Saul, whom the Philistines had killed along with his son Jonathan.[1]

It is not until much later in the story of the people of Israel, and David's reign over them, that we encounter Rizpah again. The land is parched, and the people have been starving for three years due to drought and famine. Famine was often thought to be the mark of divine judgment, so David seeks the Lord's council. The Lord says that there is a "bloodguilt" on the house of Saul because Saul had tried to wipe out the Gibeonites in violation of a prior treaty.[2] David meets with the Gibeonites and asks how he can atone for Saul's wrongdoings. The Gibeonites respond with a chilling and violent proposition: they ask that seven of Saul's sons be handed over to them to be "impaled" on a mountain top.[3] David obliges, and Rizpah's only two sons, Armoni and Mephibosheth, pay the price.

Ultimately, David sent seven sons to their deaths: Rizpah's two sons and the five sons of Merab, Saul's daughter. These seven sons are publicly executed, and their bodies are left dishonored and exposed to the heat of the day, the cold of the night, wild animals, and the human gaze. Although Rizpah's and Merab's sons are executed according to the bargain that David and the Gibeonites had struck, the famine continues.

Rizpah goes to the mountain, a piece of sackcloth serving as a symbol of her grief and mourning in hand. As a woman and a concubine to a deceased and

MOURNING FOR JUSTICE

deposed king, she has little power. In this time and place, women relied on their husbands and sons for protection and provision. Now, Rizpah has neither a husband, or sons; however, even though she could not save her sons from death, she is not entirely powerless.

Her sons are killed publicly; thus she mourns for them publicly. For six months, she sits among the bodies of her children, day after day and night after night. Is she alone, or did the women in her community bring her food and water? We may not know if other people show up, but the animals certainly do. Predators and scavengers of all kinds come to further dishonor the bodies and memories of her children. The text is silent on all the details, but it is clear that "she did not allow the birds of the air to come on the bodies by day, or the wild animals by night."[4] Rizpah stays on that mountain for months, waiting and perhaps hoping that someone will bestow on these sons the honor of a proper burial. In the meantime, all who pass need only to look up to see the rotting fruit of vengeance and violence.

When David learns of Rizpah's months-long act of public mourning, he is deeply moved and compelled to finally honor her sons. David gathers the bones of Saul and his son, Jonathan, and the bones of the seven sons, and he has them buried in the family tombs. Only then does God answer the people's prayers for rain and the flourishing of the land.

TODAY

The impact of Rizpah's mourning rippled outward from the mountaintop. It was her relentless and public grief that exposed the injustice imposed on the

[4] 2 Samuel 21:10

seven innocent sons and moved those in power to see and affirm their dignity. Mamie Till is another mother whose mourning rippled outward from a church in Chicago, even reaching down into the American South, as she grieved the gruesome and tragic murder of her son, a 14-year-old Black child.

On August 28, 1955, two white men murdered Emmett Till after he allegedly said something flirtatious to a white woman. Mamie chose to have Emmett placed in an open casket at his funeral. She could have chosen to grieve in private, perhaps only including family and dear friends in her mourning. But this mother's love for her son led her down a different path. Like Rizpah, Mamie brought her mourning out into the open. She demanded that everyone look at the beaten and bruised face of her son and see the cause of her grief and the grief of her people. Thus, Mamie's grief was exposing: she laid bare the horror and violence of racism.

Photos of Emmett's badly disfigured face were published in *Jet*, an African American magazine, and other media outlets soon picked up the story. Emmett's story is said to have been a significant early catalyst for the Civil Rights Movement. For these mothers, Mamie and Rizpah, all would see and feel their loss and the injustice that caused it. God honored their grief and brought about the beginnings of change—rain and abundance in the land for Rizpah, and the beginning of an American freedom movement for Mamie.

We will all know grief at some point, whether personally or communally. We will grieve because of death, illness, injustice, and for more reasons than can be named. Many people respond to mourning with empty positivity or platitudes—words that are insufficient for the tasks of naming our grief and holding those in the midst of it. We are told our loved ones are "in a better place" or that we should just "let go and let God." There is some kernel of truth to these ideas. There is hope of eternal life, and God is sovereign over all things.

However, Rizpah's story calls us into a different relationship with the pain and sorrow of loss. We do not have to silence or sanitize our grief. Grieving out loud and in the open can expose just how much things are not as they should be—calling out the brokenness, injustice, violence, and sin in the world. This is the power of grief. God uses the honesty of our pain to bring about change by moving others toward acts of justice and providing glimpses of the inbreaking of the kingdom of God.

Torn #1
COLT SEAGER, 2021   OIL ON COLLAGED AND TORN CANVAS

Reflect

PAUSE

Sit up straight.

Take a deep breath.

Using the art element (on the previous page),
take a moment to reflect on the story.

PONDER

Invite God to speak to you:

I.

How have you responded to your own feelings of
sorrow or grief in the past?

II.

How have you seen others respond to your grief
or the grief of your neighbors?

III.

Where do you see opportunities to bring your grief
out into the open or to stand in solidarity with those
who grieve deeply?

PRAY

God who hears,
give us the courage
to bring our sorrow
out into the open
as we wait for the day
when death and tears
will be no more.
Amen.

Tabitha

The Story of Tabitha

SYNOPSIS

Tabitha, a gifted seamstress, dies and is brought back to life as a testament to God's grace.

KEY MOMENT:
Acts 9:36–42

Read

OUTLINE

Our story begins in the wake of Tabitha's passing. A tide of grief engulfs the town of Joppa as the community mourns the loss of Tabitha—a woman of faith greatly praised and a garment maker for the poor, widowed, and vulnerable.[1] Joppa, a hub for trade, provides Tabitha with access to a wealth of materials. However, the garments she makes do more than just keep those in need warm; they are symbols of the recipients' worth and dignity, tangible expressions of love that resonate far beyond the garments themselves.

The love which Tabitha had poured into the community is returned to her in abundance. Tabitha's body is gently prepared, washed, and dressed, while the widows assemble in the upper room to pay tribute to her generous heart. Jews, who knew her as Tabitha, and Gentiles, who knew her as Dorcas, entwine their preparations in sorrow. In their own unique ways, these people all express great care for Tabitha; it is a scene of devotion that mirrors her life's work as a seamstress, as the tangible preparations are costly in time, materials, and effort.

Traditionally, death in the case of illness would have resulted in a speedy burial to protect the community and prevent the spread of disease. However, Tabitha's body lingers through the dedicated efforts of her neighbors, as if they are faithfully waiting for the Lord to intervene.

As news of her death spreads, Peter and the disciples hasten to pay their respects.[2] When Peter enters the upper room, the mourning widows proudly hold up

CREATING FOR GOOD

garments made by Tabitha, each piece a testament to her loving heart and gifted hands—articles of clothing crafted with persistence, sacrifice, and skill in a world far removed from today's disposables and fast fashion.

Upon seeing Tabitha's body, Peter sends everyone out of the room and falls to his knees in prayer. With unwavering faith, he calls out to her, "Tabitha, get up."[3] Suddenly, Tabitha's eyes flutter open, and with the help of Peter's hand, she stands up on her own two feet.[4]

When something so extraordinary happens, it can hardly be kept secret! After the miracle, Peter eagerly calls out to the community, beckoning them into the story, and he presents Tabitha to everyone—to believers and *especially* to the widows. This is a subversive act: Peter is challenging societal norms by placing women, particularly widows, first in line as witnesses.

This supernatural act doesn't just merely transform and redeem the life of Tabitha; it is a catalyst for good, sparking profound change. As a result, many people begin to believe in God, and Tabitha lives once more as God's affirmation of her life of faithfulness.[5] Her creative life's work is only just beginning, igniting a new chapter of inspiration.

Tabitha's creative faithfulness can serve as an example for today's artists. In the resurrection of her body, God affirms her life as a seamstress. But not only because she was creatively talented but also because she used her creative gifts for the sake of helping others—the poor, widowed, and vulnerable.

From the start, Tabitha is importantly described as "*always* doing kind things for others and helping the poor." Tabitha could have chosen to make clothes solely for the rich and powerful—thus selfishly using her creative talents for financial gain or social status. But instead she chooses to use her abilities and thriftiness with supplies to fashion items for the vulnerable in her community. In this way, she makes things of *truly* lasting importance—uniquely generated heirlooms of economic, personal, and spiritual value. Her craft is both timeless and enduring for those most in need.

Tabitha's story offers us a powerful reminder that our ability to create is deeply spiritual and an expression of our faith. Even more importantly, it challenges us to ask *who* we are creating for. How can we use our artistic gifts and resources to create beauty and bring dignity to those in need? We all have the ability to make something truly meaningful; may it be so.

The Pearl
SAMUEL HAN, 2022   **DIGITAL PHOTOGRAPH**

Reflect

Sit up straight.

Take a deep breath.

Using the art element (on the previous page),
take a moment to reflect on the story.

PONDER

Invite God to speak to you:

I.

Who are the artists in your life? What does their
craft display about God's character?

II.

How do you express yourself creatively? What relationship does your creativity have with the world
around you?

III.

What ways can our creativity bring value to our
communities?

PRAY

Creator God,
You make all things new.
Guide my craft
to serve my community.
May my creativity
bring value and beauty.
And may it all
be for your glory.
Amen.

Thomas

The Story of Thomas

HOPE AGAINST ALL ODDS

SYNOPSIS

Thomas struggles to believe in the impossible—a resurrected Jesus—until he witnesses it firsthand.

KEY MOMENT:	FULL READING:
John 20:24-29	John 20

Read

Two nights after Jesus's death, the disciples gather together. Only Thomas is absent. It is dangerous for them to be seen all together, so they lock the door to the room they are in. They had decided to meet because earlier that day, Mary Magdalene had come running to Peter and John, saying that she had seen Jesus in the flesh! "Could this be true?" they wondered. As if he had heard them, Jesus comes into the room through the locked door and stands before them. To show them that it is really him in the flesh, he shows them the wounds in his hands, sides, and feet—markers of the gruesome execution they had all witnessed.

When they next see Thomas, they tell him what happened. But Thomas had just seen Jesus crucified with his own eyes. Thomas knows that Jesus is dead! We can only imagine what was running through Thomas' mind—are his friends delusional? Desperate?

Thomas just couldn't believe without proof. After all, for the last three years, Thomas had hoped Jesus was the Messiah his people had been waiting for. With no meaningful socio-political changes, in Thomas' mind, Jesus turned out to be nothing more than a normal man lying dead in his grave, quickly defeated by the very powers he had claimed to come to defeat. He tells his friends firmly, "Unless I see the nail marks in his hands, put my finger in the wounds left by the nails, and put my hand into his side, I won't believe!"[1] He will not give in to the delusion.

A week passes, and Jesus doesn't come back to see the group. For a whole week, Thomas is alone as the only person in Jesus's inner circle who hasn't seen him in the flesh. Listening to his friends' certainty, we

HOPE AGAINST ALL ODDS

can imagine there is something in him that wants to believe. There is something inside of him that pushes him to have hope against all odds. But what if he gives in, places his hope in this impossible resurrection, and ends up being wrong again?

The next day, Thomas and the disciples gather once more. They had locked the door; but just as he had before, Jesus appears in the room with them. This time, Jesus speaks directly to Thomas. As if he had heard what Thomas said to the disciples the week before, Jesus shows Thomas his hands and tells him to touch the nail holes. He shows Thomas his side and tells him to put his hands inside the wound. "Now, no more doubt!" Jesus says firmly, "Believe!" [2]

Thomas looks at Jesus. He sees the wounds scabbed over with dried blood; he sees his chest rise and fall with each breath; he sees the color rise in his cheeks as he speaks. Thomas realizes it is true—his Master is alive! He breathes out his shock—and maybe his relief—saying, "My Lord and my God!" That is all he can say, but it is enough. "Doubting Thomas" may have been the last disciple to believe the resurrection. But once he sees Jesus, resurrected and in the flesh, he is the first person to dare call Jesus not just Christ, or Lord, but God incarnate. [3]

TODAY

Thomas' relationship with hope and doubt is something that many of us can resonate with in a society that constantly changes. His story gives us cause to hope for a better future; at the same time, however, it shows us that, in our journey towards hope, doubt may inevitably creep in. We can experience hope on a societal scale, such as when a medical breakthrough

[2] John 20:27 / [3] John 20:28

is made or new resources are given to a disadvantaged community; we can experience hope on a personal level as well, like when we receive a new job, start a fresh relationship, or witness the birth of a child.

Sometimes these events really do change everything for the better. At other times, however, they fall short—maybe the medical breakthrough ends up failing or the new relationship ends up hurting us—and we have to live with disappointment clouding our ability to hope for anything better. If we find ourselves in this kind of disillusionment, how could we ever find hope again?

Thomas was in a similar position; in the midst of his despair and disappointment over Jesus's death, his friends told him the impossible—they had seen Jesus! Thomas couldn't bear to hope that what they said was true. Jesus let Thomas sit in his disbelief— his pain—for a full week before he appeared to him. When he finally saw Jesus, Thomas recognized him not only as the human he knew, but, for the first time, also as God—something no one else had dared say out loud this directly before. His hope, against all odds, was not in vain.

The same is true for us in our complex circumstances. The things we hope for don't always happen as quickly as we would like—nor do they always go as planned. We, like Thomas, may find ourselves in despair or grief over our unrealized hopes. But the story of Jesus is a story of the impossible coming true. It inspires us to maintain our hope against all odds. It shows us that Jesus' power will meet us in large and small ways, and it provides us with clarity and optimism we didn't have before. Thomas is known as a "doubter," but his story invites us to embrace hope.

White Terraces

CHARLES BLOMFIELD, 1882

OIL ON CANVAS

Reflect

Sit up straight.

Take a deep breath.

Using the art element (on the previous page),
take a moment to reflect on the story.

PONDER

Invite God to speak to you:

I.

What are some unrealized dreams in your life?
What does it look like to maintain hope?

II.

How does Jesus inspire us to embrace hope and
open ourselves to change in our own lives and the
world around us?

III.

How can we nurture and cultivate a deeper sense
of trust in the unknown?

PRAY

God of the Impossible,
when disappointment clouds
and dampens our dreams,
may we trust
in your power.
Sustain our hope.
Amen.

The Widow and Her Coins

The Story of the Widow and Her Coins

SYNOPSIS

A poor widow who is burdened by the injustice of a religious offering system is encouraged by Jesus' loving attention and his affirmation of God's fairness.

KEY MOMENT:	FULL READING:
Mark 12:41-44	Mark 12

Read

OUTLINE

A woman hesitantly enters the Temple's courts to make her contribution. Mark uses two words to describe this woman: poor and widow. Each conveys her loss and vulnerability.

Jesus had been teaching here earlier, and things are still bustling as the widow enters the Court of Women—the innermost court where women are allowed to gather. She presses toward the collection box alongside the others bringing their offerings.

She clenches two small coins in her fist[1]—the smallest coins at the time, like pennies. She slows her pace, knowing these coins are everything she has to live on. While not enough to purchase everything she needs, it's at least something.

Seared into her memory are times when the Temple authorities scolded her, saying that monetary donations are a required mark of faithfulness. This never sat right with her, though. She would think to herself, "When I leave my offerings, I am left with nothing. When the wealthy leave their contributions, they still have more than they need. Why would God approve a system like this?"

She notices Jesus sitting near the collection box, watching as people make their offerings. Deep down, she knows it's unfair. At the same time, she has always been taught to trust the Temple's religious authorities. And she loves God and wants to be obedient.

So, she continues forward.

[1] Mark 12:41-42

SHARING OUR RESOURCES / GIVING

People's metal coins clink against the bronze collection container as they drop in, the sound proclaiming the amount of each contribution. Men in stylish robes and jewelry drop several heavy coins into the treasury,[2] the loud sound announcing the largeness of their gifts.

We can imagine the widow's breath catches as she releases her coins into the container, with sounds barely audible as they drop. She walks away, wondering what to do now that she has nothing, and tries to suppress the hot tears of desperation and frustration rising up. She notices Jesus' eyes on her as she heads toward the area for women's prayer. Within his gaze she senses loving attentiveness, yet also some sadness.

She hears Jesus call his followers to him and explain that what they just witnessed is deeply unjust.[3] He points out what the woman herself had felt: wealthy people gave large donations, but truthfully, were not negatively affected in any way. In contrast, she, a poor widow, had been compelled to give the only money she had to live on and was left with nothing.

Her heart swells, and she feels a sense of vindication with Jesus' words. He confirms the truth that God is indeed loving, fair, and just, even if the Temple leaders and this system of giving is not.

The disciples also recognize the wisdom in Jesus' words, and connect this situation to what he said earlier that day: that religious leaders are only pretending to be pious, all the while cheating vulnerable widows out of their property.[4]

The woman had been coming to the Temple her whole life, but this was the first time she felt truly seen and honored there.

[2] Mark 12:43-44 / [3] Mark 12:43 / [4] Mark 12:38-40

Generously sharing our resources with our community can be a meaningful way to live out our relationship with God. But as we learn from the widow, these contributions do not happen in a vacuum. They are connected to beliefs and values that have been nurtured in us, and exist alongside our unique life circumstances.

Since the birth of the Church, Christian communities have been sustained by the time, talents, and resources of their members. Sadly, some communities exploit these offerings. Some even use this history to coerce people to give in ways that leave them depleted.

Reflect on how you were taught about the importance of giving in the Christian life, and which values defined these practices.

God is a God of abundance, and gives us good gifts. With those gifts comes an invitation to be generous, both for our joy to care for our neighbors, and to grow in faithfulness and trust. There may be times when we feel compelled to give sacrificially, and in those moments, we can take time to discern whether that call is coming from God, or from leaders or a structure that requires more than what is right.

The widow invites us to see and honor the humanity of every person making a contribution; and that includes ourselves. When we compare what we give to what others give, or sense others making this comparison, we can pause and remember that while the contributions we offer are important to Jesus, who we are underneath is even more important to him.

More Than Enough
SAMUEL HAN, 2023   **DIGITAL PHOTOGRAPH**

Reflect

PAUSE

Sit up straight.

Take a deep breath.

Using the art element (on the previous page),
take a moment to reflect on the story.

PONDER

Invite God to speak to you:

I.

What values and beliefs have shaped your understanding of giving and generosity?

II.

Have you ever felt pressured to give more than you were comfortable with, whether by religious leaders or other influences? How did you respond?

III.

In what ways can we ensure that our contributions to our communities are made out of genuine joy and a sincere desire to care for others, rather than coercion or obligation?

PRAY

God who gives,
we give thanks
for your good gifts.
Help us to give,
to resist pressures,
and to resist false piety.
In your ways,
may justice
and compassion abound.
Amen.

The Woman Caught in Adultery

The Story of The Woman Caught in Adultery

SYNOPSIS

A woman is publicly shamed by religious leaders, but is met with compassion by Jesus, freeing her from shame and empowering her to live with grace.

SHAME

KEY MOMENT:	FULL READINGS:
John 8:1-11	John 7:14–8:11

Read

All eyes are on her, at the moment in her life when she least wants them to be. It all happens so fast. One moment she is in private, alone with a man who is not her husband; the next, she is being dragged against her will into the public square—and to the temple, of all places.[1]

Strangers' hands—she realizes they are not just any strangers' hands, but those of the religious leaders in her community[2]—grab hold of her and push her along. They didn't take the man she was with. They have no interest in shaming him publicly, only her.

Shame, at the hands of religious leaders. Shame, in the place where religion is practiced.

A rabbi is teaching in the Temple courts, and large crowds have come to hear him.[3] It is these crowds whose eyes now turn toward her, as the religious leaders shove her in the middle of the courts, in front of everyone.

Shame, in front of a large, large crowd.

The religious leaders tell the lone rabbi that the law of Moses says that this woman should be put to death by stoning.[4] Despite their roughness and clear lack of concern for her wellbeing, as she looks in their eyes, she doesn't exactly see bloodlust. Instead, she sees cold calculation in their gaze.

SHAME

They don't necessarily want to kill her—although they would be willing to do so if it seemed to serve their purposes. They simply don't care about her experience. Their attention is focused on the upstart rabbi, Jesus. They have brought her there to try to trap him, to try to get him to say something considered blasphemous.[5]

Shame, so much shame, and all for the purpose of a conflict that has nothing to do with her.

Jesus does not take the bait. Instead of responding, he bends over and starts drawing with his finger in the dirt.[6] The woman feels the crowd's attention shift from her shame to his unexpectedly crouched-over figure.

As the religious leaders continue questioning Jesus, he finally picks himself up off the ground. His voice is soft but clear, as he makes eye contact with each one who looks at him: "The one of you who is without sin, let them throw the first stone."[7]

Jesus turns the question of sin, the exposure of shame, away from her and onto the religious leaders who have brought her there. She holds her breath. Are any of them without sin—that is, have any of them always done right by God, themselves, and their community at every point in their lives? Do any of them *think* they are without sin—do they really think they had never harmed another person with their words or actions?

[5] John 8:6 / [6] John 8:6 / [7] John 8:7

A long moment passes, and then one of the religious leaders—a very old man—slowly begins to walk away, his head bowed. Then another older man, and another. Eventually, some of the younger ones. As Jesus keeps writing, they all leave.[8]

Shame, draining away from her. Shame, passing from her onto the ones who shamed her.

"Did no one condemn you?" Jesus asks. It is the first time since being pushed into the middle of the temple court that the woman is invited to speak, the first time anyone cares what she has to say. She answers, "No one, Lord."[9]

Jesus replies, "Neither do I condemn you; go, and from now on, no longer sin."[10]

Jesus has no interest in shaming her. He does not condemn her. And if he doesn't, then surely the religious leaders have no right to. Jesus doesn't even weigh in on the question of whether the woman is a sinner or what punishment her sin might deserve. He just says, in essence, *from now on, do right by yourself, God, and others. There is no condemnation for you. No shame. Only grace. Go live in that grace.*

Shame, replaced by grace, by healing, by freedom.

SHAME

I do not condemn you. These are powerful words for anyone who has experienced shame.

Some of us may relate to the experience of being intentionally and publicly shamed, just like the woman. Certainly, all of us have made mistakes; we have all done things we regret. Many of us might even have aspects of our identities, physical appearances, histories, or personalities that we feel ashamed of, or that our society considers shameful.

Shame doesn't only come from sources outside ourselves. It can also be an internal voice that says, *You aren't good enough. There's something wrong with you. If they really knew you, they would reject you. Make yourself smaller. Hide.*

Our shame can keep us from connecting in healthy, authentic ways with other people—but Jesus wants to free us from our shame.

If Jesus does not condemn us for who we are or what we've done, who else has the right to do so? Jesus invites us to be accountable for our actions, to make things right where we can, to "go and no longer sin."

But Jesus does not want us to sit mired in shame over our mistakes, and he certainly does not want us to be ashamed of who God created us to be. Jesus doesn't want us to be shamed by other people, and he doesn't want us to be devastated by internalized shame either. This is good news indeed.

On the flip side, then, Jesus also has something to say to those who feel the urge to condemn or shame others. *Let the one who is without sin throw the first stone.* These, too, are powerful words.

Jesus takes a situation on the precipice of violence—a scene that comes uncomfortably close to ending in a gory public mob execution—and diffuses it nonviolently. He sows seeds of peace by inviting the would-be condemners to look within themselves.

We can—and should—speak out against injustice and condemn harmful ideas, theologies, and policies. But we are not to condemn people. Violence is not ours to enact. We are not to throw stones. Jesus shows us a better way, a way in which shame is replaced by grace and violence is replaced by peacemaking.

Surrounded
BETH WOLFE, 2018   SCREEN PRINT

Reflect

Sit up straight.

Take a deep breath.

Using the art element (on the previous page),
take a moment to reflect on the story.

PONDER

Invite God to speak to you:

I.

Have you ever felt overburdened by shame, either
from external sources or from within yourself?
How did this impact your relationships with yourself, others, and God?

II.

How can we practice extending grace to ourselves
and others, rather than defaulting to condemnation, judgment, or shame?

III.

How can we balance accountability for our actions
and recognizing that we aren't defined by mistakes?

PRAY

Merciful God,
thank you for grace
and for the freedom
from shame.
As we seek accountability
and meet others' needs,
help us to see your Image
in all of us.
Amen.

SHAME

The Women Who Follow Jesus

Discipleship

The Story of The Women Who Follow Jesus

SYNOPSIS

A diverse community of women joins Jesus on his journey to spread the Gospel—united in their shared desire to grow and be transformed into a new kind of community marked by justice, love, and mutuality.

KEY MOMENT:	FULL READING:
Luke 8:1-3	Luke 8:1-21

DISCIPLESHIP

Read

When Jesus travels from village to village to proclaim the good news of the kingdom of God,[1] he doesn't just speak to large crowds. He also—slowly and deliberately—gathers around himself a community. This community of intentional learners—often called disciples, which in the original Greek comes from the word for learning (*mathetes*)—accompanies Jesus in his journey. They are united by a deep desire to grow, to be formed and transformed, and to learn from this rabbi about how to live.

The gospel writer Luke is careful to remind us that these disciples include women. As Jesus travels and preaches, heals and casts out demons, feeds and instructs, the twelve named male disciples are with him.[2] But it isn't just the Twelve who follow him. There are also many others, women and men alike. The community of learners includes Mary Magdalene, Joanna, and Susanna—along with many other women Luke doesn't name.[3]

No two of these female disciples are exactly alike. Some are married, like Joanna, the wife of Chuza, while others are single, as Mary Magdalene seems to be. Some are materially comfortable; others live in poverty. Many are wealthy enough to support Jesus' traveling ministry out of their own pockets.[4] Each woman gives what she can so that the community can flourish.

Some of these women follow Jesus because he has cast demons out of them.[5] Others follow Jesus because he sees and honors their faith.[6] For others still, he affirms their desire to sit at his feet and learn in the midst of a world that expects them to always be busy serving.[7]

[1] Luke 8:1 / [2] Luke 8:1 / [3] Luke 8:2-3 / [4] Luke 8:3 / [5] Luke 8:2 /
[6] The "sinful" woman in Luke 7:36-50 / [7] Mary in Luke 10:38-42

Many are likely captivated by Jesus' stories about seed scattered in good soil;[8] when they had heard these stories, they knew he invited them—just as much as he had invited the men in their world—to treasure his words deep in their hearts, to live out his teachings fruitfully. No doubt some are drawn to Jesus' redefinition of family: *my mother and brothers are those who hear God's word and put it into practice.*[9]

In the community Jesus aims to build, female disciples are entirely equal to male ones. The same is true for disciples from different ethnic groups, for those who are wealthy and those who are materially poor, and for those who are married and those who are single. Jesus teaches people to form a new kind of community together—connected by their desire to know and love God, and by their commitment to listen to Jesus about who God is, what God is like, and what God wants for humans.

No one is to rule over anyone else.[10] Everyone is to come as a learner. Everyone is to bring what they have to offer, to be open to new relationships and to new kinds of relationships—relationships marked by justice, love, and mutuality.

TODAY

In his letters to the early churches, the apostle Paul often speaks of Christian community as a kind of body. Each part of this body has a function that is essential to the whole. Likewise, when Jesus made disciples, they were not all meant to be the same. Jesus was not interested in shaping everyone he met into a singular mold of what a godly human should be.

Jesus was interested in people's growth, building communities, and teaching ways of living. He made room

[8] Luke 8:4-15 / [9] Luke 8:19-21 / [10] Luke 22:24-26

for people to become disciples in different ways, to follow him for different reasons, and to be healed in different ways. He wanted people to become the unique individuals God made them to be, and to form the kind of community God wants to see. Faithful discipleship can differ depending on our social location—all of the characteristics, such as gender, race, and class, that influence how others see us and determine the kinds of privileges and opportunities that are accessible to us. Some social locations carry more power than others.

For everyone to be able to exercise their role in the body fully and freely, as equals, some people might need to step up while others need to step back. For some of the women in Luke's story, discipleship meant stepping forward, putting themselves out there, letting everyone know how they had been healed, and bravely stepping up to participate as equals with men in a new kind of community.

For the Twelve and the other men, this may have been challenging. It may have been humbling to receive financial support from women,[11] and they may have felt resentful when women crashed their male-dominated dinner parties and Jesus didn't mind one bit.[12] They likely weren't accustomed to learning together with women. All these things differed from the norms of their patriarchal world.

But all these things were good for the women and the men. The whole community benefited from hearing women's perspectives and insights as they learned together, from seeing women's boldness and faith in approaching Jesus, and from witnessing women's experiences of God. Jesus frees us to become disciples in our own ways, and to see the myriad forms discipleship takes as beautiful. Together, as a community of disciples, we are whole.

[11] As in Luke 8:3 / [12] Luke 7:36-50

Small Red Blossoms on a Vine
KATSUSHIKA HOKUSAI, 1830

DRAWING ON THIN HANDMADE PAPER :
INK WASH, COLOR

Reflect

PAUSE

Sit up straight.

Take a deep breath.

Using the art element (on the previous page),
take a moment to reflect on the story.

PONDER

Invite God to speak to you:

I.

Jesus encouraged his disciples to be lifelong learners, always seeking to grow and transform. How
can we embrace a spirit of learning and growth
in our own lives?

II.

How can we create communities in which everyone can exercise their role fully and freely?

III.

How can we create an environment that encourages individuals to embrace their unique paths and
motivations in their journey towards discipleship?

PRAY

God,
we come to you as learners.
Help us to see
the beauty in our diversity,
and to honor each other
fully and freely.
Guide us in building a community
in which no one is ruled over or silenced,
but all are welcome
to grow and flourish.
Amen.

Zacchaeus

The Story of Zacchaeus

SYNOPSIS

Zacchaeus, a despised tax collector, is transformed by an encounter with Jesus and encouraged to right his wrongs.

KEY MOMENT:
Luke 19:1-10

Read

Our story takes place in the ancient city of Jericho, which is nestled in an oasis north of the Dead Sea in the arid Jordan Valley. This bustling metropolis is Zaccheus' home and the base of operations for his lucrative career as a tax collector.

His chosen profession is rightly despised by the Israelites. Not only does he cooperate with the oppressive Roman Empire to extract punishing taxes from his fellow Jews, Zacchaeus has become wealthy through the common but shady practice of charging higher fees and funneling the difference into his glamorous estate.

But Zacchaeus is more than a corrupt government bookkeeper. He is the *chief* tax collector, a high-ranking official likely in charge of the entire region. He isn't simply complicit in an unjust system—he is its architect.

We don't know what compels Zacchaeus to go looking for Jesus that day. Perhaps he is merely celebrity spotting, drawn to the buzz surrounding this unusual Nazarene and the miracles he leaves in his wake. Maybe he is curious about the self-proclaimed Messiah, a figure long-awaited by every Jew—even traitorous ones. Perhaps he senses something deeper and more mysterious, a tug of conviction, a restlessness, an unexplainable but unmistakable gut feeling.

Whatever his motives, Zacchaeus, given his short stature, is enthusiastic enough to hike up his fine clothing and scramble up a sycamore tree in the hopes of seeing Jesus with his own eyes. This plan goes even better than he anticipates, for Jesus immediately spots him and calls out to him by name.

"Zacchaeus! I *must* stay at your house today."[1] Must. To Jesus, dinner with Zacchaeus is a necessity—almost as if this is the very purpose for his visit. So, he invites himself over and Zacchaeus eagerly welcomes him.

The crowds, however, are less enthused. They grumble at the attention Jesus is bestowing upon Zacchaeus, a man so marked by corruption he is dubbed a "notorious sinner."[2] Their confusion is understandable and not without merit, for Jesus has many choice words (and whips)[3] for those who take advantage of the poor and marginalized. Yet here he is, sharing dinner with a known perpetrator in a house built on the backs of those he cheated.

They have seen this man inflict harm on their community for years. Clearly, Zacchaeus is selfish, set in his ways, and beyond hope. So why does Jesus make time for him? He seems to be wasting his energy at best and condoning his actions at worst. What redeeming qualities could Jesus possibly see in him?

But they barely make it home before Zacchaeus shocks everyone with a surprise announcement. He stands before Jesus and pledges half his possessions to the poor and makes a promise to repay everyone he has cheated fourfold.

We'll never know what was said to convince Zacchaeus or if Jesus' presence was enough to strike his heart with conviction, but this joyous display of repentance will always be a reminder that even the most stalwart of sinners can change.

In response, Jesus declares Zaccheus' house a "home of salvation" and calls him a "true son of Abraham"—his faith was credited to him as righteousness. This story ends with the reminder that Jesus came to

[1] Luke 19:5 / [2] Luke 19:7 / [3] John 2:13-16 / [4] Luke 19:9-10

"seek and to save the lost."[4] Though Zacchaeus has strayed far from God, Jesus knows exactly how to spot him among the branches and call him in.

The story of Zacchaeus is refreshing in a culture full of half-hearted apologies and empty promises made by out-of-touch public figures. While many seem pressured to release statements to clean up their image, Zacchaeus models for us genuine repentance, which includes a plan of action to repair harm. He also avoided the pitfall of performatively wallowing in his mistakes, which can pull attention away from the victims. Instead, he simply identified what he did wrong and declared what he would do to fix it.

When we recognize our faults or are held accountable by others, it can be difficult to accept. Often, it's a shock to our self-image, and we struggle to reconcile the light and dark parts of ourselves. Our first instinct may be to act defensively: making excuses, rationalizing our decisions, or even shrugging off responsibility altogether. Like the religious expert in Luke 10:29, we may be tempted to over-intellectualize basic kindness by asking, "Who is our neighbor?" We may walk away weeping from a challenge to change our ways, as the rich young man did in the previous chapter of Luke.[5]

We all have faults, but it's what we do next that matters. Zacchaeus shows us that it's possible to repent with joy. Rather than allowing shame to crush us, we can treat accountability as a freeing opportunity to make things right with God and others. Rather than bemoaning how justice can complicate our lives, we can answer Jesus' call to build a radically different kingdom. And though we must grapple with the ways in which we stray from God's path, we can also celebrate how Jesus persistently calls us back onto the road of restoration.

RIGHTING OUR WRONGS

[5] Luke 18:23

Figuurstudie van een man met tulband en zwaard
RADEN SALEH, 1824-1880   **PENCIL, WATERCOLOR**

Reflect

PAUSE

Sit up straight.

Take a deep breath.

Using the art element (on the previous page),
take a moment to reflect on the story.

PONDER

Invite God to speak to you:

I.

How can we shift our mindset from shame and de-
fensiveness to joy and repentance when faced with
our faults and mistakes?

II.

In what areas of our lives do we feel compelled to
take responsibility for our actions and make things
right with God and others?

PRAY

God,
may I own up
to my mistakes
and take action
to repair harm.
Teach me to repent
with joy, not shame—
to correct wrongdoings
against You and others.
Amen.

Zipporah

The Story of Zipporah

SYNOPSIS

Zipporah holds a deep understanding of God's ways, despite her outsider status, and uses her knowledge to protect her family and respond to God's actions.

KEY MOMENT:	FULL READING:
Exodus 4:25-26	Exodus 4

EMBODIED KNOWLEDGE

Read

OUTLINE

Zipporah, a Midianite woman, is introduced to us in Exodus 2. She is a daughter of a Midianite priest, a sister to six other women, and is married to Moses. The Midianites were foreigners to the Hebrew people and had a mixed reputation with the Israelites. Exodus 4 gives us more insight into Zipporah, who is also a keeper of knowledge and rituals of YHWH. We may never understand what happened in Exodus 4:24–26, and perhaps many of the ancient Israelites did not either—Moses certainly did not. We may also find the details of this story jarring, confusing, and even disturbing. However, we can see that while others had forgotten, Zipporah knew and carried with her the knowledge of God.

At the beginning of our story in Exodus 4, an odd encounter occurs: God seeks to kill Moses. Shortly before these events, Moses had met God in a burning bush on a mountain in or near Midian and received a call to speak on God's behalf to the Hebrew people and to the Pharaoh of Egypt. Moses is called to return to Egypt and declare, and even facilitate, YH-WH's liberation of the enslaved Hebrew people.

After receiving a blessing from his father-in-law, Moses packs up with Zipporah and their son Gershom to return to Egypt. One night during the journey, YHWH comes to kill. While the text is ambiguous, Moses appears to be the target. Reminiscent of Jacob meeting and wrestling with God at Bethel, it seems that God wrestles with Moses, but with the intent of mortal harm.

Zipporah, seeing this, grabs a flint, cuts the foreskin off her son, and rubs the bloody foreskin on "his" feet. Suddenly, YHWH releases Moses. There are numerous ambiguities here. We don't know on whose feet Zipporah rubs the blood. Gershom's? Moses's? YHWH's? Additionally, in the Hebrew Bible, feet can refer to legs or euphemistically to genitals. Where did Zipporah rub the blood? Perhaps most puzzlingly, why is God seeking to kill Moses, the very person God had just commissioned in the first place? Has he sinned against God? Is he not circumcised and thus not ritually prepared to serve as YHWH's ambassador? The text provides no answer. Why does this ritual cause YHWH to release Moses? Does the blood atone for some wrongdoing? Does circumcision fulfill some requirement? Does the blood work like the blood the Hebrew people smeared on their door frames in Exodus 11–12, which allowed God to "Passover" their houses and not kill their firstborn children? We will never know. Moses himself doesn't seem to know. Most importantly, however, Zipporah knows.

The mysteries of this event and YHWH's behavior are clear to Zipporah. She not only understands what God is doing, but she also knows the rituals and practices necessary to respond to YHWH's actions and to protect herself and her family from harm. While Exodus does not refer to Zipporah as a priestess, she clearly seems to have a deep and embodied priestly knowledge, despite her lack of an official religious title. She is a keeper of the ways of YHWH.

TODAY

Zipporah is an educator. Exodus 1–2 introduces us to the Hebrew people after they had undergone generations of enslavement in Egypt. With the passing of time, it is clear that the Hebrew people have forgotten the God of Abraham, Isaac, and Jacob—they no longer remember God's name, nor the practices associated with worshipping this God. In Exodus 19,

Zipporah's father, the priest of Midian, offers the first burnt offerings and sacrifices to YHWH for the freed Israelite people, passing along knowledge about how to offer sacrifice. In Exodus 4, Zipporah performs the first circumcision for the Israelites, communicating the knowledge of this ritual. Zipporah teaches Moses how to live in relation to YHWH, just as her father will.

The story of Zipporah should remind us to be mindful of our assumptions about who possesses religious authority and who does not. How could the Hebrew people learn about YHWH from the Midianites? In Numbers and Judges, the Midianites are considered foreign enemies of the Hebrew people. Yet, in the book of Exodus, every encounter with YHWH is supported by an interaction with the Midianites, and they are the ones who safeguard the knowledge of YHWH and share it with the newly freed Israelites. Understanding our own spirituality may come through an unexpected person or tradition. We also may be that unexpected person for another.

Zipporah demonstrates how knowledge is embodied and exists beyond certifications and degrees. This is not an argument against knowledge that is institutionally recognized, but a reminder that knowledge is just as likely to be found outside of these institutions as it is within. Many of us, on account of race, ethnicity, gender, sexuality, wealth, beliefs, age, or any number of identifiers, have our knowledge and judgment discounted until verified by an individual with the proper accolades; however, Zipporah reminds us that our knowledge does count. For those of us with titles, certifications, or expertise, Zipporah teaches us to be humble and to listen for what we need to learn. The pastor must listen to the congregation, the teacher must learn from the student, and the parent must see through the child's eyes.

EMBODIED KNOWLEDGE

Billow-by
JACKIE TAM, 2018

ETCHING

Reflect

Sit up straight.

Take a deep breath.

Using the art element (on the previous page), take a moment to reflect on the story.

PONDER

Invite God to speak to you:

I.

What does "embodied knowledge" mean to you? What role have you played in passing along knowledge, values, or traditions to others?

II.

How does the story of Zipporah challenge our assumptions about religious and ethnic authority?

III.

List your common sources of spiritual knowledge. In what ways have you encountered unexpected sources of spiritual or religious knowledge?

PRAY

Oh, Creator God,
giver of all knowledge,
teach us to love
our bodies,
learn from our neighbors,
and to seek the divine
in all things.
Amen.

EMBODIED KNOWLEDGE

ALABASTER

TYLER ZAK
Product & Branding Director

DARIN MCKENNA
Content Editor & Coordinator

SAMUEL HAN
Art Director

RACHEL CHANG
Layout Designer

ECHO YUN CHEN
Cover Image

BRYAN YE-CHUNG
Co-Founder, Creative Director

BRIAN CHUNG
Co-Founder, Managing Director

WILLA JIN
Finance & Talent Director

EMALY HUNTER
Operations & Customer Experience Director

EMMA TWEITMANN
Senior Marketing Coordinator

MINZI BAE
Senior Marketing Coordinator

ALABASTER

STORY

WRITERS	ARTISTS
Darin Mckenna	Bryan Ye-Chung
Aaron Dorsey	Julia Signe
Nick Peterson	Wesleigh Byrd
Chris Lopez	Erin Clark
Darin Mckenna	August Macke
Emma Tweitmann	Jackie Tam
Liz Cooledge Jenkins	Arkhip Ivanovich Kuidzhi
Ruth Schmidt	Julia Signe
Josh Hilton	Colt Seager
Zac Calvo	Edward Theodore Compton
Zac Calvo	David Kakabadzé
Bryan Ye-Chung	Walter de Navazio
Haley Black	Jonathan Todryk
Bethany McKinney Fox	Ľudovít Čordák
Darin Mckenna	Menci Clement Crnčić
Tamisha Tyler	Johann Walter-Kurau
Ruth Schmidt	Bryan Ye-Chung
Chris Tweitmann	Jackie Tam
Matthew Hayashida	Jonathan Todryk
Katie McEachern	Walter de Navazio
Joel Yoshonis	Pedro Figari
Chris Tweitmann	Helene Schjerfbeck
Teesha Hadra	Colt Seager
Mattea Gernentz	Samuel Han
Bethany McKinney Fox	Charles Blomfield
Liz Cooledge Jenkins	Samuel Han
Liz Cooledge Jenkins	Beth Wolfe
Katie McEachern	Katsushika Hokusai
Adrian Patenaude	Raden Saleh
Aaron Dorsey	Jackie Tam

ENDNOTES

ADAM & EVE

- Brueggemann, Walter. *Genesis: Interpretation: A Bible Commentary for Teaching and Preaching.* Louisville, KY, Westminister John Knox Press, 2010.
- Carr, David McLain. *The Hebrew Bible: A Concise, Contemporary Introduction. 2nd ed.,* Hoboken: Wiley, 2020.
- Gafney, Wilda. *Womanist Midrash: A Reintroduction to the Women of the Torah and the Throne.* First edition. Louisville, KY, Westminster John Knox Press, 2017.
- Trible, Phyllis. *God and the Rhetoric of Sexuality.* Overtures to Biblical Theology 2. Philadelphia, Fortress Press, 1978.

BALAAM

- Angelou, Maya. Interview by Oprah Winfrey. *The Oprah Winfrey Show.* Harpo Productions, 1995.

THE BLEEDING WOMAN

- Brown, Brené. *Braving the Wilderness: The Quest for True Belonging and the Courage to Stand Alone* (Random House reprint edition, 2019) 14.

HULDAH & JOSIAH

- West, Cornel. *Democracy Matters: Winning the Fight Against Imperialism.* Penguin Press, 2004.
- West, Cornel. *Race Matters.* Beacon Press, 1993.

MARY

- Bonhoeffer, Dietrich. *The Mystery of the Holy Night: Thoughts on the Words of the Christmas Liturgy.* Translated by Jana Riess, The Crossroad Publishing Company, 1999, p. 17.

THE PRISON GUARD

- Nouwen, Henri J.M. *The Wounded Healer: Ministry in Contemporary Society.* Doubleday, 1979.

ZIPPORAH

- Ackerman, Susan. *Why Is Miriam Also Among the Prophets? (And Is Zipporah Among the Priests?).* Journal of Biblical Literature vol. 121, no. 1, 2002, pp. 47–80.
- Allen, Ronald B. *The 'Bloody Bridegroom' in Exodus 4:24–36.* Bibliotheca Sacra, no. 153 (September 1996), pp. 259–69.
- Childs, Brevard S. *The Book of Exodus: A Critical, Theological Commentary.* 2004.
- Dozeman, Thomas B. *Commentary on Exodus.* The Eerdmans Critical Commentary. Grand Rapids, MI, W.B. Eerdmans Pub. Co, 2009.
- Gafney, Wilda. *Womanist Midrash: A Reintroduction to the Women of the Torah and the Throne.* 1st. ed., Louisville, Kentucky, Westminster John Knox Press, 2017.
- Winslow, Karen S. "Ethnicity, Exogamy, and Zipporah." *Women in Judaism: A Multidisciplinary Journal* vol. 4, no. 1, Winter 2006.

CONTINUE THE CONVERSATION

www.alabasterco.com